THE JOY OF SNACKS

Nancy Cooper, R.D.

Diabetes Center, Inc. Minnetonka, Minnesota

Library of Congress Cataloging-in-Publication Data

Cooper, Nancy.
The joy of snacks.

Includes index.
1. Snack foods—Composition—Tables. 2. Food—Composition—Tables. 3. Diabetes—Nutritional aspects.
I. Title.
TX551.C754 1987 613.2 86-24178
ISBN 0-937721-18-2

Acknowledgements

Without the talents of the following people, this book would not have been possible. I would like to thank Neysa Jensen for editing the book; Ann Larson for recipe testing and development; Mary Ann Roeder for typing; Linda Lundborg for her assistance in layout and design; Tom Foty for the illustrations; Marion Franz, R.D., M.S., Arlene Monk, R.D., Diane Reader, R.D., Broatch Haig, R.D., and Gay Castle, R.D. for reviewing the book; Donnell Etzwiler, M.D., Bill Henry, and the entire staff of the International Diabetes Center for their support and encouragement.

I also wish to thank the many friends and clients of the IDC who contributed several of their own recipes for use in this book.

Nancy Cooper
Diabetes Nutrition Specialist
International Diabetes Center

TABLE OF CONTENTS

Snack /snăk/ n: a light meal: food eaten between regular meals.

For years, snacking was considered unhealthy. Parents tried to prevent their children and teenagers from eating between meals, and adults refused snacks in order to control weight.

Today, that has all changed, and you may be surprised to learn that snacking can actually be good for you! In fact, snacks can supply your body with nutritious foods that your regular meals may be lacking.

SNACKING FOR EVERYONE

Snacking has almost become a way of life. It occurs everywhere--at work or school, at meetings and parties, at athletic events, at movies, and at home. To many people, snacking offers a flexible eating plan that matches a busy lifestyle. In addition, snacks help some people meet their nutritional requirements.

CHILDREN

Young children are often unable to consume all the food they need in three square meals a day. Children's calorie needs are often as great as those of adults, but their stomachs are smaller, so they really need to eat every three to four hours. Snacks can be an important supplement to a child's diet. They should be small but satisfying, and should be offered at specific times during the day (about 1 1/2 to 2 hours before meals).

To ensure that children receive nutrition along with their snacks, parents need to determine what is and is not allowed at snack time. This does not mean that children should never indulge in a sweet treat (we are all born with a natural liking for sweetness), but they should not learn that every meal must end with cookies, cake, or pie or that every time they are hungry between meals they should have a sweet.

Better snack choices for kids are fruit (dried, fresh, or canned without sugar); cut up raw vegetables served with peanut butter, cheese, or cottage cheese; whole grain breads or crackers with peanut butter, cheese, or milk; dry cereal with milk (look for varieties that are not coated in sugar); popcorn; and fruit or vegetable juices. To satisfy a child's sweet tooth, try serving cookies or quick breads, muffins, or any of the other desserts found in this book that are prepared with less sugar and fat.

TEENS

Snacking is also important for teenagers and adolescents. Busy schedules and a need for independence lead to more food choices out of the home and a pattern of eating "on-the-run." The adolescent years are also a time of rapid growth and increased physical activity, calling for an adjustment in calorie and nutrient needs. Snacks may provide up to 25% of a teenager's calories, so it is important they be selected from a wide variety of foods that offer the most nutrition for the calories they contain.

ADULTS

Adults enjoy snacking for many reasons. For some people a snack provides a needed break in the day's routine at work or home. Eating regular snacks also helps control the appetite and decrease the amount of food eaten at meals.

It is not true, as many people believe, that eating between meals causes weight problems. In fact, there is no direct connection between body weight and the number of times an individual eats during the day. All food, no matter when it is eaten, contains a certain number of calories. Weight gain results only when a person consumes more calories than the body uses for energy.

As you can see, for optimal weight control, calories must be controlled at meals as well as snacks, and the number of times a person eats in a day is not as important as what is eaten. Snacking actually helps people to lose weight because it eliminates hunger pangs during the day and allows individuals to eat smaller meals while still satisfying the appetite.

Elderly people, individuals who live alone, and people with small appetites will also benefit from eating smaller amounts of food more frequently during the day. Many senior citizens find snacking an important social and recreational part of their lives. People who live alone find it easier to prepare several light snacks during the day rather than three large meals.

For all people, however, correct selection of snacks is important to meet the daily required nutrients for energy and good health. The chart shows the recommended number of servings from each of the major food groups. Snacks should be planned to supplement food eaten at meals to ensure daily nutritional requirements are met.

Food Group	Recommended Number of Servings				
	Child	Teenager	Adult	Pregnant Woman	Lactating Woman
Milk 1 cup milk, yogurt, OR **Calcium Equivalent:** 1½ slices (1½ oz) cheddar cheese* 1 cup pudding 1¾ cups ice cream 2 cups cottage cheese*	3	4	2	4	4
Meat 2 ounces cooked, lean meat, fish, poultry, OR **Protein Equivalent:** 2 eggs 2 slices (2 oz) cheddar cheese* ½ cup cottage cheese* 1 cup dried beans, peas 4 tbsp peanut butter	2	2	2	3	2
Fruit-Vegetable ½ cup cooked or juice 1 cup raw Portion commonly served such as a medium-size apple or banana	4	4	4	4	4
Grain, whole grain, fortified, enriched 1 slice bread 1 cup ready-to-eat cereal ½ cup cooked cereal, pasta, grits	4	4	4	4	4

*Count cheese as serving of milk OR meat, not both simultaneously.

"Others" complement but do not replace foods from the Four Food Groups. Amounts should be determined by individual caloric needs.

SNACKING AND DIABETES

If you have diabetes, snacks are an important part of your meal plan. For children, adolescents, and adults with insulin dependent (Type I) diabetes, snacks help prevent fluctuations in blood glucose (sugar) levels. Between meal and bedtime snacks are planned for peak times of insulin activity and for times of physical activity.

For individuals with non-insulin-dependent (Type II) diabetes, snacks provide a way to distribute calories evenly during the day to help the body's insulin work better and blood glucose (sugar) levels to remain more stable. Eating smaller meals with between meal snacks also helps people with diabetes control their appetite and may make weight loss easier.

SNACKS AND DENTAL CAVITIES

Carbohydrate is a nutrient in food necessary for a balanced diet. Many nutrients in carbohydrate-containing snacks, such as vitamin D and calcium (present in milk products), are important for the development of strong teeth and bones. All carbohydrates--starches and sugars--can cause dental plaque buildup on teeth whether eaten as a snack or as a meal. Bacteria in the plaque produce an acid which can dissolve tooth enamel and begin the process of tooth decay. The stickiest forms of carbohydrate (such as candy, caramel, and syrups) that remain in contact with the teeth for a long period of time contribute the most to the formation of dental cavities.

To preserve teeth from cavity formation, choose carbohydrate snacks low in sticky, refined sugars, such as milk and plain yogurt, fresh fruit and vegetables, crackers, popcorn, cereal, and other grain products. Good oral hygiene habits including regular visits to the dentist and brushing and/or flossing teeth after meals and snacks is also important.

SNACKS AND SODIUM

Chips, pretzels, salted nuts, and cheese curls—all popular snack foods—have one thing in common: they are all very salty. Unfortunately, Americans like salty food. People with high blood pressure, or hypertension, need to limit salt in their diets, and a moderate salt intake for most other Americans is also recommended. Although an occasional serving of a higher sodium snack food is acceptable, these foods should be used in moderation, since they frequently contain significant levels of calories and fat as well as sodium. Although most recipes in this book contain acceptable levels of sodium, a few do have more than 400 mg. per serving. If your dietitian or doctor has recommended that you limit sodium, we suggest you use those recipes with higher sodium levels less often. For further information on low sodium eating, consult ***Pass the Pepper Please!***

SNACKS: YOUR CHOICE

Snacking is indeed a way of life. Now that you know the important nutrient contribution snacks can make to your diet, choose snacks appropriately to add variety to your eating pattern. Snacking can be fun, enjoyable, and good for you!

About the Recipes

The recipes in *The Joy of Snacks* have been developed according to the Dietary Guidelines for Americans. These guidelines suggest ways to choose and prepare foods to keep you and your family as healthy as possible:

1. Eat a variety of foods
2. Maintain desirable weight
3. Avoid too much fat, especially saturated fat and cholesterol
4. Eat foods with adequate starch and fiber
5. Avoid too much sugar
6. Avoid too much sodium
7. If you drink alcoholic beverages, do so in moderation

These recommendations apply to all Americans, including those with diabetes and cardiovascular disease, making these recipes useful for all people interested in a healthy diet.

Recipe Modifications

All of the recipes in *The Joy of Snacks* have been modified to reduce calories, saturated fat, cholesterol, sodium, and refined sugar. There are two ways to modify a recipe: change a cooking technique or change an ingredient. One way to change a cooking technique is to bake rather than fry, thereby reducing total fat and calories. An ingredient may be modified by reducing the amount used, eliminating it completely, or by substituting a more acceptable ingredient. Substituting plain lowfat yogurt for sour cream or reducing the amount of sugar in a muffin recipe are examples of how to modify ingredients.

Many substitutions can be made in recipes to lower the fat, sugar, or salt content. While the taste and texture may be slightly changed, the results are still very appealing. *Opening the Door to Good Nutrition* contains many tips to help you modify your recipes.

Consider using these recipe modifications in your own recipes:

Recipe Modifications

For Lowering Total Fat, Saturated Fat, and Cholesterol

For	Try
1 whole egg	1/4 cup egg substitute or 1 egg white plus 1 teaspoon vegetable oil or 2 egg whites
1 cup butter	1 cup margarine
1 cup shortening or lard	3/4 cup vegetable oil
1/2 cup shortening	1/3 cup vegetable oil
1 cup whole milk	1 cup skim milk
1 cup light cream	1 cup evaporated skim milk or 3 tablespoons oil plus skim milk to equal 1 cup
1 cup heavy cream	1 cup evaporated skim milk or 2/3 cup skim milk plus 1/3 cup oil
1 cup sour cream	1 cup plain lowfat yogurt or 1 cup lowfat cottage cheese, blended with 2 tablespoons lemon juice until creamy
1 ounce regular cheese	1 ounce skim milk cheese
2 tablespoons flour (as thickener)	1 tablespoon cornstarch
1 tablespoon salad dressing	1 tablespoon low-calorie salad dressing
1 ounce (1 square) baking chocolate	3 tablespoons powdered cocoa plus 1 tablespoon oil
1 can condensed soup	Homemade skim milk white sauce (1 cup skim milk + 2 tablespoons flour + 2 tablespoons margarine)
cream of celery	1 cup sauce + 1/4 cup chopped celery
cream of chicken	1 1/4 cups sauce + 1 chicken bouillon cube
cream of mushroom	1 cup sauce + 1 can drained mushrooms
1 ounce bacon (2 strips)	1 ounce lean Canadian bacon or 1 ounce lean ham
cream cheese (1 ounce)	Neufchatel cheese (1 ounce)

Reprinted from *Opening the Door to Good Nutrition.*

Pointers on Ingredients

The recipes in this book use common household ingredients. These hints will help ensure your cooking success:

- Read product labels. Food labels contain important bits of information that will help your recipes turn out the way you expect them to. Some recipes call for foods with a specific calorie content or specific nutritional guidelines. These facts can be found on product labels. If you read labels carefully, you will save time and money, and your recipes will be successful.
- The herbs used in these recipes are dried unless otherwise noted. If you are using fresh herbs, substitute approximately three times the amount indicated (e.g., 3 teaspoons chopped fresh basil for 1 teaspoon dried basil leaves).
- When using frozen bread dough, look for the whole wheat variety to increase the fiber content of the recipe.
- Unless otherwise noted, the peanuts used in the recipes are skinless.
- If a recipe calls for oil, use a polyunsaturated vegetable oil such as safflower, sunflower, corn, soybean, or cottonseed.
- When using margarine, look for a brand that lists a liquid vegetable oil as the first ingredient on the label. The stick form of margarine should be used in cooking. Soft tub margarines will not cream. Diet margarines contain more water and less fat, so they cannot be substituted ounce per ounce for regular stick margarine or butter.
- Use unsifted flour unless otherwise noted.
- Evaporated skim milk must be very cold or partially frozen before it will whip. The mixing bowl and beaters should also be chilled.
- Several recipes call for Equal brand sweetener in place of sugar. Equal brand sweetener is available in single serving packets. One packet (one teaspoon) is as sweet as 2 teaspoons of sugar but supplies only 4 calories.

  Equal can be used to sweeten foods and beverages in which you would normally use table sugar. It can be used only in recipes which do not require heating, because the sweetener loses its sweetness when exposed to heat. In addition, the sweetener does not provide the necessary bulk and structure required in home-baked foods such as breads, muffins, and cookies (and therefore, cannot completely replace sugar). In these foods, sugar is a necessary ingredient. However, the recipes in this book for muffins, breads, and cookies use less sugar than the original recipes. If you have diabetes, these particular foods with sugar should be used in small portions only on an occasional basis.

Remember to allow cooked fruits and fruit sauces to cool before sweetening with Equal brand sweetener. Mousses, puddings, gelatins, chilled desserts, ice cream, and sherbert can also be sweetened with Equal.

- Some recipes that require cooking call for a saccharin-containing sweetener, which comes in several forms. Liquid non-caloric sweeteners may be added directly to the food mixture. Non-caloric sweetening tablets may be crushed and stirred into liquid mixtures, or they may be dissolved first in a small amount of liquid called for in the recipe and then added to the rest of the mixture. Granulated non-caloric sweeteners may be added in the same way sugar would be added in a recipe.

  In cooking with saccharin, it is generally best, if possible, to add the sweetening agent toward the end of the cooking process or immediately afterwards. Saccharin tends to turn bitter tasting after exposure to high temperatures for a long period of time (as in baking).
- Salt is essential in breads. Without it, they may not rise at the appropriate rate. Salt has been eliminated or reduced in recipes where used solely for flavor, but it remains in recipes where necessary for the cooking process.

Cooking Tips for Success

To guarantee your satisfaction with these recipes, consider these hints for preparation.

- Read each recipe thoroughly before you begin. Since all recipes have been modified, cooking methods and ingredients may be unfamiliar to you.
- Measure and/or weigh all ingredients carefully.
- When dissolving gelatin over heat, use low heat and stir constantly, since gelatin burns easily.
- When dissolving arrowroot, flour, or cornstarch in liquid, add the dry ingredients to the liquid, not vice versa, to avoid clumping.
- Cooking times on most recipes are approximate. Many variables affect cooking time, such as the temperature of the food before it is cooked, the type of heat used for cooking, and the type of cookware you are using. To ensure positive results, check frequently for doneness.
- When baking in muffin tins, partially fill any empty muffin cups with water to prevent the pan from burning or warping.

- If a food is chilled or frozen after cooking, allow it to cool slightly before refrigerating or freezing.
- Allow baked muffins and breads to cool before cutting or slicing to avoid crumbling.
- Use vegetable oil or an aerosol vegetable spray for coating pans and muffin tins before baking.
- Ovens should be preheated for 10 minutes unless otherwise noted. If you do not preheat, allow approximately 5 to 10 minutes additional cooking time.

Nutrition Information

Each recipe in this book contains nutrition information for one serving including calories, grams of carbohydrate, protein, fat and milligrams of sodium. Sugar, when used in recipes, has been calculated into the total carbohydrate content, and most recipes contain less than one teaspoon of sugar per serving.

You will also find the food exchange value based on *Exchange Lists for Meal Planning.* Food exchanges provide a simple way of monitoring calories and nutrients eaten at meals and snacks. For more information on the exchange lists, please see the appendix, page 268.

If a given serving size is too large for your meal plan, you can divide the serving size and the listed calculations to give you a more appropriate portion. Similarly, the serving size, calculations, and exchange values may be multiplied to accommodate a larger portion.

It is hoped that *The Joy of Snacks* will inspire you to enjoy preparing and eating healthy foods. The recipes have been tested, tasted, and retested, resulting in a collection of foods that can be enjoyed by you, your family, and anyone you cook for. It may be "diet food" to some people, but it is good food for all!

Here's to eating well and living well.

1.
THE JOY OF APPETIZERS

Whether you call them hors d'oeuvres, antipasto, canapes, or zakuski, the appetizers in this section are sure to whet the appetite and excite the senses.

Traditional appetizers are usually high in fat and calories because of the butter, sour cream, and mayonnaise used. Many of the recipes here substitute plain lowfat yogurt at 10 calories per tablespoon, compared with 100 calories per tablespoon for butter or mayonnaise. Other lower calorie and lower fat ingredients used in this section include light cream cheese, water-packed canned salmon and tuna, reduced calorie mayonnaise, and part-skim mozzarella cheese.

Use these appetizers as snacks, light meals, or as a great beginning to a full-course dinner.

Salmon Cheese Ball

1 15 1/2-ounce can water-packed salmon
8 ounces light cream cheese
2 teaspoons horseradish
2 teaspoons chopped green onion
1/4 teaspoon salt
1/2 teaspoon lemon juice
Chopped parsley

YIELD: 1 1/3 cups
SERVING SIZE: 2 tablespoons
PER SERVING: Calories-138
Carbohydrate-1 g.
Protein-11 g.
Fat-10 g.
Sodium-trace
EXCHANGES: 1 1/2 medium-fat meat, 1/2 fat

Drain salmon, removing any bones and skin. Pat dry on paper towel; flake into bowl. Add remaining ingredients, except parsley; stir to blend thoroughly. Form into ball in bowl. Cover. Chill 2 to 3 hours or overnight. Remove from bowl, sprinkle with chopped parsley. Place on serving plate: surround with crackers or crisp fresh vegetables.

Honey Peanuts

1 1/2 tablespoons honey
1 teaspoon grated orange rind
1/2 teaspoon vanilla
1 cup dry-roasted peanuts (not Spanish)

YIELD: 1 cup
SERVING SIZE: 2 tablespoons
PER SERVING: Calories-181
Carbohydrate-9 g.
Protein-9 g.
Fat-14 g.
Sodium-138 mg.
EXCHANGES: 1/2 fruit, 1 high-fat meat, 1 fat

Combine honey, orange rind, and vanilla. Add peanuts; stir until evenly coated with honey mixture. Spread peanuts on oiled baking sheet, one layer deep. Bake at 350° for 8 to 10 minutes or until lightly browned. Immediately after removing from oven, spread peanuts on plate or flat pan to cool. Store in airtight container.

Great for munching!

Peanut Butter Sticks

8 slices bread
1 cup chopped peanuts
1/2 cup peanut butter
1 tablespoon oil

YIELD: 24
SERVING SIZE: 1
PER SERVING: Calories-85
Carbohydrate-6 g.
Protein-4 g.
Fat-6 g.
Sodium-96 mg.
EXCHANGES: 1/2 starch/bread, 1 fat

Trim crusts from bread. Cut bread slices in thirds. Place bread and crusts on a baking sheet and bake at 150° for 30 minutes or until dry. Place crusts in blender and whirl until finely crumbled. Combine bread crumbs with chopped nuts. Heat peanut butter and oil over low heat, until mixture is thin. Dip bread slices in peanut butter, then roll in nut/crumb mixture. Dry on baking sheet. Store in airtight container.

This is delicious made with raisin bread.

Cheesy Tuna Pita

1 pita bread
6 tablespoons Terrific Tuna Dip (see recipe page 64)
2 tablespoons part skim mozzarella cheese

YIELD: 2
SERVING SIZE: 1
PER SERVING: Calories-115
Carbohydrate-11 g.
Protein-9 g.
Fat-4 g.
Sodium-200 mg.
EXCHANGES: 1 starch/bread, 1 lean meat

Separate pita bread in half. Spread 3 tablespoons Terrific Tuna Dip on each half. Top with 1 tablespoon mozzarella cheese. Broil until cheese melts; fold over for sandwich. Serve immediately.

Pita Bread Snackers

1 pita bread
4 teaspoons plain lowfat yogurt
1 teaspoon Italian herbs
1/2 cup Terrific Tuna Dip (see recipe page 64)

YIELD: 4
SERVING SIZE: 2
PER SERVING: Calories-108
Carbohydrate-12 g.
Protein-8 g.
Fat-3 g.
Sodium-400 mg.
EXCHANGES: 1 starch/bread, 1 lean meat

Separate pita bread in half. Cut each half into 2 pieces making a total of 4 pieces. Spread each piece with 1 teaspoon yogurt and sprinkle with 1/4 teaspoon Italian herbs. Broil until edges are brown. Spread 2 tablespoons Terrific Tuna Dip on each pita piece. Serve immediately.

Quick Bread Sticks

1 7 1/2-ounce can refrigerated biscuits
1 1/4 cups crisp rice cereal, coarsely crushed
1/2 teaspoon salt
3 tablespoons skim milk
1 1/2 tablespoons grated Parmesan cheese

YIELD: 20
SERVING SIZE: 2
PER SERVING: Calories-100
Carbohydrate-14 g.
Protein-2 g.
Fat-4 g.
Sodium-29 mg.
EXCHANGES: 1 starch/bread, 1 fat

Cut each biscuit in half. Roll each half into a 5-inch stick. Combine rice cereal and salt. Roll each stick in milk and then in cereal. Place on baking sheet and sprinkle with Parmesan cheese. Bake at 400° for 8 to 10 minutes or until golden brown.

For Peanut Butter lovers!

Spicy Chicken Fingers

4 boneless chicken breast halves, skinned
2 tablespoons plain lowfat yogurt
15 soda crackers, crushed
1 teaspoon dried thyme
1/2 teaspoon dried marjoram
1/4 teaspoon curry powder
salt, to taste
Sauce:
1/2 cup plain lowfat yogurt
2 tablespoons catsup
2 tablespoons finely chopped celery
2 teaspoons soy sauce
1/2 teaspoon finely chopped garlic, optional
1/4 teaspoon ground black pepper

YIELD: 24
SERVING SIZE: 2
PER SERVING: Calories–53
Carbohydrate–2 g.
Protein–9 g.
Fat–1 g.
Sodium–68 mg.
EXCHANGES: 1 lean meat

Trim visible fat from chicken; cut each breast into 6 even strips. Coat chicken pieces with yogurt. Combine cracker crumbs, thyme, marjoram, and curry. Roll chicken strips in crumbs. Place chicken in single layer on cake rack set in baking pan. Bake at 375° for 25 minutes or until crumbs are lightly browned and crisp. Remove from oven. For sauce, combine yogurt, catsup, celery, soy sauce, garlic, if desired, and pepper to taste. Serve as dip for chicken fingers.

Zucchini Pizza Slices

3 medium zucchini, sliced
1 6-ounce can tomato paste
36 thin pieces (1 1/2 inch square) part skim mozzarella cheese
1/3 cup grated Parmesan cheese
Mixed Italian herbs, crumbled

YIELD: 36
SERVING SIZE: 1
PER SERVING: Calories-30
Carbohydrate-2 g.
Protein-3 g.
Fat-2 g.
Sodium-43 mg.
EXCHANGES: 1 vegetable

Parboil zucchini in boiling water for 1 minute or until crisp and tender; remove with slotted spoon; drain on paper towels. Place zucchini in a single layer on a baking sheet. Top each with 1 teaspoon tomato paste and a slice of mozzarella cheese. Sprinkle with 1/2 teaspoon Parmesan cheese and top with herbs.

Broil 4 inches from heat for 3 minutes or until cheese is melted and zucchini is heated through. Serve hot.

Denver Pizza Snacks

1 11-ounce package refrigerated French loaf dough
1 tablespoon prepared mustard
1 cup diced cooked ham
1/2 cup chopped onion
1/2 cup chopped green pepper
2 medium tomatoes, diced
1 cup chopped fresh mushrooms
6 ounces shredded part skim mozzarella cheese
2 teaspoons dried oregano
1 teaspoon dried basil
freshly ground black pepper to taste

YIELD: 12
SERVING SIZE: 1
PER SERVING: Calories-140
Carbohydrate-14 g.
Protein-10 g.
Fat-4 g.
Sodium-360 mg.
EXCHANGES: 1 starch/bread,
1 medium-fat meat

Preheat oven to 375°. Oil bottom of 13 x 9 inch pan. Fit dough into bottom of pan, trimming edges as needed. Bake dough 6 to 7 minutes. Remove from oven. Spread with mustard. Layer ham, onion, green pepper, tomatoes, mushrooms, cheese, herbs, and ground pepper over bread. Bake until cheese is bubbly, 20 to 25 minutes. Cut into 12 squares. Serve warm.

Pizza Snacks

4 Triscuit brand crackers
4 tablespoons pizza sauce or tomato sauce
1/2 ounce sliced meat (cut into bite-sized pieces)
1/2 ounce part skim mozzarella cheese

YIELD: 4
SERVING SIZE: 4
PER SERVING: Calories-184
Carbohydrate-18 g.
Protein-10 g.
Fat-8 g.
Sodium-410 mg.
EXCHANGES: 1 starch/bread, 1 medium-fat meat, 1/2 fat

Spread pizza sauce or tomato sauce on crackers. On each one place a slice of meat and a slice of cheese. Heat in 325° oven until cheese melts.

Italian-Style Nibble Mix

1/4 cup unpopped popcorn
2 cups toasted oat cereal
2 cups bite-sized shredded wheat squares
2 tablespoons margarine, melted
1/4 cup grated Parmesan cheese
1 tablespoon dry Italian salad dressing mix

YIELD: 9 cups
SERVING SIZE: 1/2 cup
PER SERVING: Calories-60
Carbohydrate-9 g.
Protein-1 g.
Fat-2 g.
Sodium-118 mg.
EXCHANGES: 1 starch/bread

Pop corn in heavy skillet or saucepan over medium-high heat using little or no oil. Cover skillet and shake pan constantly until all corn is popped. In 13 x 9 x 2 inch baking pan, combine popcorn, oat cereal, and wheat squares. Heat at 300° for about 5 minutes. Remove. Drizzle with margarine. Combine cheese and salad dressing mix, sprinkle over snack mix, and stir. Serve warm.

Temptation Snack Mix

4 cups bite-size shredded wheat squares
1 cup unsalted peanuts
2 cups pretzel sticks
1/4 cup margarine
1 1/2 teaspoons basil
2 tablespoons grated Parmesan cheese
1 1/2 teaspoons oregano
1/2 teaspoon garlic powder

YIELD: 7 cups
SERVING SIZE: 1/2 cup
PER SERVING: Calories-170
Carbohydrate-18 g.
Protein-5 g.
Fat-9 g.
Sodium-296 mg.
EXCHANGES: 1 starch/bread, 2 fat

In large bowl, combine cereal, peanuts, and pretzel sticks. In small saucepan over low heat, combine margarine, basil, Parmesan cheese, oregano, and garlic powder. Pour over cereal mixture while stirring; blend well. Spread mixture on a 15 x 10 inch baking pan. Bake at 325° for 20 minutes, stirring after 10 minutes. Cool. Store in an airtight container.

Traditional Chex® Party Mix

1/3 cup margarine
1 1/4 teaspoons seasoned salt
4 1/2 teaspoons Worcestershire sauce
2 2/3 cups Corn Chex cereal
2 2/3 cups Rice Chex cereal
2 2/3 cups Wheat Chex cereal
1 cup salted mixed nuts

YIELD: 9 cups
SERVING SIZE: 1/2 cup
PER SERVING: Calories-121
Carbohydrate-14 g.
Protein-3 g.
Fat-7 g.
Sodium-301 mg.
EXCHANGES: 1 starch/bread, 1 fat

Preheat oven to 250°. Heat margarine in large shallow roasting pan (15 x 10 x 2 inches) in oven until melted. Remove. Stir in seasoned salt and Worcestershire sauce. Add cereals and nuts. Mix until all pieces are coated. Heat in oven 1 hour, stirring every 15 minutes. Spread on absorbent paper to cool. Store in airtight container.

Microwave directions: In large bowl melt margarine on high for 1 minute. Stir in seasoned salt and Worcestershire sauce. Add cereals and nuts. Mix until all pieces are coated. Microwave on high for 6 to 7 minutes, stirring every 2 minutes. Let cool and store in airtight container.

Jumble Party Mix

1/4 cup creamy peanut butter
1/4 cup margarine
1/4 teaspoon salt
1/4 teaspoon garlic powder
2 1/4 teaspoons Worcestershire sauce
4 cups Rice Chex cereal
4 cups Wheat Chex cereal
3/4 cups unsalted peanuts
1 cup raisins

YIELD: 9 cups
SERVING SIZE: 1/2 cup
PER SERVING: Calories-157
Carbohydrate-21 g.
Protein-4 g.
Fat-7 g.
Sodium-241 mg.
EXCHANGES: 1 1/2 starch/bread, 1 fat

Preheat oven to 250°. Melt peanut butter with margarine in large shallow roasting pan (15 x 10 x 2 inches) in oven until shiny and soft, about 5 minutes. Remove. Stir in salt, garlic powder, and Worcestershire sauce until mixture is blended. Add cereals and nuts. Mix until all pieces are coated. Bake in oven 1 hour. Stir every 15 minutes. Remove from oven. Stir in raisins. Spread on absorbent paper to cool. Store in airtight container.

Party Snack Mix

1/2 cup margarine
1 teaspoon salt
1 teaspoon garlic salt
4 teaspoons Worcestershire sauce
2 cups Rice Chex cereal
2 cups Corn Chex cereal
2 cups Bran Chex cereal
1 cup pretzels
2 cups corn nuts

YIELD: 9 cups
SERVING SIZE: 1/2 cup
PER SERVING: Calories-125
Carbohydrate-16 g.
Protein-1 g.
Fat-6 g.
Sodium-476 mg.
EXCHANGES: 1 starch/bread, 1 fat

Heat oven to 250°. Melt margarine in saucepan. Remove from heat, add salt, garlic salt, and Worcestershire sauce. Combine cereals. Pour margarine mixture over cereal and toss. Add pretzels and corn nuts; toss until all pieces are coated. Bake for 45 minutes in large shallow baking pan, stirring occasionally. Cool completely and store in an airtight container. (Note: To reduce sodium content, eliminate salt and substitute 1/4 teaspoon garlic powder for the garlic salt.)

Crispy Chips

1 pita bread
4 teaspoons margarine, softened
2 1/2 tablespoons grated Parmesan cheese

YIELD: 8
SERVING SIZE: 2
PER SERVING: Calories-76
Carbohydrate-6 g.
Protein-2 g.
Fat-4 g.
Sodium-132 mg.
EXCHANGES: 1/2 starch/bread, 1 fat

Separate pita bread in half. Cut each half into four sections. Spread 1/2 teaspoon margarine on each section. Sprinkle each with 1 teaspoon Parmesan cheese. Broil until edges are brown. Serve hot.

Variation: Substitute 1/8 teaspoon garlic or onion powder for Parmesan cheese.

Taco-Rific

1 avocado, peeled, pitted, and cut into chunks
1/2 cup plain lowfat yogurt
1/2 cup reduced calorie cream cheese
3/4 teaspoon taco seasoning

YIELD: 1 3/4 cups
SERVING SIZE: 2 tablespoons
PER SERVING: Calories-48
Carbohydrate-2 g.
Protein-1 g.
Fat-5 g.
Sodium-41 mg.
EXCHANGES: 1 fat

Whirl all ingredients in blender until smooth and well blended. Serve in bowl with chips or with crisp vegetables. This dip can also be spread on a lettuce leaf and rolled up like a jelly roll.

Cheesy Artichokes

1 14-ounce can artichokes, 6 to 8 count
1/2 cup reduced calorie mayonnaise
1/2 cup shredded part skim mozzarella cheese
1 tablespoon grated Parmesan cheese
paprika
chopped parsley

YIELD: 32
SERVING SIZE: 1
PER SERVING: Calories-40
Carbohydrate-1 g.
Protein-1 g.
Fat-3 g.
Sodium-57 mg.
EXCHANGES: 1 fat

Thoroughly drain artichokes and pat dry on paper towel. Cut each into quarters. Arrange artichokes in 8-inch round baking dish. Combine mayonnaise, mozzarella cheese, and Parmesan cheese. Spread over artichokes. Sprinkle with paprika. Bake at 325° for 15 to 18 minutes until edges are brown. Sprinkle with chopped parsley. Serve a quartered artichoke on cracker or spear with cocktail toothpicks. Serve hot.

Cheese Nibbles

1/2 cup margarine, softened
1/2 cup shredded part skim mozzarella cheese
1/2 cup shredded cheddar cheese
1/4 teaspoon Worcestershire sauce
1 cup all-purpose flour
1 cup crisp rice cereal

YIELD: 60
SERVING SIZE: 1
PER SERVING: Calories-64
Carbohydrate-4 g.
Protein-2 g.
Fat-4 g.
Sodium-96 mg.
EXCHANGES: 1 fat

Stir together margarine, mozzarella cheese, cheddar cheese, and Worcestershire sauce. Add flour and rice cereal. Stir thoroughly. Roll dough into 60 marble sized pieces. Place on baking sheet and bake at 350° for 8 to 10 minutes. Cool slightly on baking sheet before removing.

23. THE JOY OF BEVERAGES

Club soda is not the only beverage choice for the person who wants to control calories! This section contains a wide variety of refreshing and creative drinks to satisfy any appetite, age, or occasion. Many are flavored with sugar-free carbonated sodas and fruit juices. You will find thick, creamy malts (with plain lowfat yogurt instead of ice cream) and beverages suitable for entertaining.

Try adding a colorful, edible garnish to your beverages: fruit-filled ice rings or cubes, lemon or lime slices, mint leaves, or frozen cubes of fruit juice.

The next time you reach for a club soda, mix a Frosty Peach Cooler, Champagne Surprise, or Lemon Fizz instead!

Orange Juice Cocktail

2 tablespoons lime juice
4 ounces unsweetened orange juice
liquid artificial sweetener (equal to 1 teaspoon sugar)
4 ounces club soda

YIELD: 10 ounces
SERVING SIZE: 10 ounces
PER SERVING: Calories-70
Carbohydrate-17 g.
Protein-1 g.
Fat-trace
Sodium-1 mg.
EXCHANGES: 1 fruit

Mix all ingredients and serve over ice in tall glass. Serves 1.

Orange Summer Cooler

1 cup unsweetened orange juice
3/4 cup crushed ice or 6 ice cubes
1/2 cup unsweetened fresh or frozen strawberries
1 banana
1 packet Equal brand sweetener

YIELD: 2 3/4 cups
SERVING SIZE: 2/3 cup
PER SERVING: Calories-61
Carbohydrate-15 g.
Protein-1 g.
Fat-trace
Sodium-1 mg.
EXCHANGES: 1 fruit

Whirl all ingredients in blender for 30 to 60 seconds. Pour into tall glasses. Serves 4.

So Easy Fruit Cooler

3/4 cup crushed ice or 6 ice cubes
1 peeled orange, cut into chunks
1 banana, cut into chunks
1 12-ounce can sugar-free ginger ale

YIELD: 2 1/4 cups
SERVING SIZE: 3/4 cup
PER SERVING: Calories-61
Carbohydrate-15 g.
Protein-1 g.
Fat-trace
Sodium-26 mg.
EXCHANGES: 1 fruit

Whirl first 3 ingredients in blender until ice is dissolved. Add ginger ale and whirl again. Pour into tall glasses. Serves 3.

Peach Yogurt Fizz

1 cup unsweetened sliced peaches
1 cup plain lowfat yogurt
1/2 cup nonfat dry milk powder
1 packet Equal brand sweetener
4 ounces club soda

YIELD: 3 cups
SERVING SIZE: 1 cup
PER SERVING: Calories-135
Carbohydrate-21 g.
Protein-10 g.
Fat-2 g.
Sodium-146 mg.
EXCHANGES: 1 skim milk, 1/2 fruit

Whirl peaches, yogurt, milk powder, and sweetener in a blender until smooth. Pour into three glasses and add club soda to top. Serve immediately. Serves 3.

Frosty Peach Cooler

1 fresh ripe peach, peeled and sliced
1/4 teaspoon lime juice
1/4 cup water
3 tablespoons unsweetened frozen orange juice concentrate
1/2 cup crushed ice
1 12-ounce can sugar-free lemon-lime flavored carbonated beverage

YIELD: 3 1/2 cups
SERVING SIZE: 3/4 cup
PER SERVING: Calories-37
Carbohydrate-9 g.
Protein-1 g.
Fat-trace
Sodium-1 mg.
EXCHANGES: 1/2 fruit

Whirl peach slices, lime juice, water, orange juice concentrate, and crushed ice in blender until smooth and frosty. Pour over ice cubes in tall glass until half full. Fill with carbonated beverage and stir gently. Serves 5.

Ginger Peach Fizz

1 12-ounce can sugar-free lemon-lime flavored carbonated beverage
1/4 teaspoon ginger
1 1/2 cups fresh peaches, peeled and chopped
2 tablespoons lemon juice
2 packets Equal brand sweetener

YIELD: 3 cups
SERVING SIZE: 1 cup
PER SERVING: Calories-38
Carbohydrate-9 g.
Protein-1 g.
Fat-trace
Sodium-16 mg.
EXCHANGES: 1/2 fruit

Whirl all ingredients in blender until smooth. Pour over ice cubes. Serves 3.

Easy Lemonade

3 tablespoons lemon juice
1 cup cold water
1/4 cup unsweetened pineapple juice concentrate
1 packet Equal brand sweetener

YIELD: 12 ounces
SERVING SIZE: 6 ounces
PER SERVING: Calories-64
Carbohydrate-15 g.
Protein-trace
Fat-trace
Sodium-trace
EXCHANGES: 1 fruit

Mix all ingredients together and pour over ice. Serves 2.

Lemon Fizz

6 ice cubes
Liquid artificial sweetener to equal 6 teaspoons sugar
1/3 cup lemon juice
10 ounces club soda
2 slices lemon

YIELD: 2 cups
SERVING SIZE: 1 cup
PER SERVING: Calories-10
Carbohydrate-3 g.
Protein-trace
Fat-trace
Sodium-25 mg.
EXCHANGES: Free

Crush ice cubes and divide between two 10-ounce glasses. Dissolve sweetener in lemon juice, then pour 2 1/2 tablespoons of mixture on top of crushed ice in each glass. Pour 5 ounces club soda into each glass and stir briskly. Cut lemon slices halfway through to core and garnish side of each glass.

Orange Slush

1 cup unsweetened orange juice
2 tablespoons plus 1 teaspoon lemon juice
4 packets Equal brand sweetener
1/3 cup nonfat dry milk powder
1/3 cup ice water

YIELD: 2 1/4 cups
SERVING SIZE: 3/4 cup
PER SERVING: Calories-69
Carbohydrate-13 g.
Protein-3 g.
Fat-trace
Sodium-40 mg.
EXCHANGES: 1 fruit

Combine orange juice, 2 tablespoons lemon juice, and sweetener. Pour into 1-quart ice tray. Freeze until slushy. Beat dry milk powder and ice water in small mixer bowl until soft peaks form. Beat in 1 teaspoon lemon juice. Add orange juice mixture while beating at low speed. Freeze again in ice tray until almost firm, stirring occasionally. Serve with spoons or short straws. Serves 3.

Strawberry Lemon Slush

1 12-ounce can sugar-free lemon-lime flavored carbonated beverage
1 cup fresh strawberries, sliced
1 teaspoon lemon juice
crushed ice

YIELD: 3 cups
SERVING SIZE: 1 cup
PER SERVING: Calories-18
Carbohydrate-4 g.
Protein-trace
Fat-trace
Sodium-trace
EXCHANGES: free

Whirl all ingredients in blender until smooth. Pour into tall glasses. Serves 3.

Daiquiri Dream

1/4 small banana
1/2 cup unsweetened apple juice
3 ice cubes
1/2 cup unsweetened orange juice
1 tablespoon lemon juice

YIELD: 1 1/2 cups
SERVING SIZE: 1/2 cup
PER SERVING: Calories-48
Carbohydrate-12 g.
Protein-1 g.
Fat-trace
Sodium-1 mg.
EXCHANGES: 1 fruit

Combine all ingredients in blender and whirl until ice cubes are crushed. Serves 3.

Champagne Surprise

1/3 cup unsweetened apple juice, chilled
1/4 teaspoon lemon juice
club soda, chilled

YIELD: 6 ounces
SERVING SIZE: 6 ounces
PER SERVING: Calories-40
Carbohydrate-10 g.
Protein-trace
Fat-trace
Sodium-trace
EXCHANGES: 1 fruit

Chill a champagne glass or wine glass. Pour apple juice and lemon juice into a measuring cup. Add enough club soda to make 3/4 cup; stir gently to blend. Pour into glass and serve immediately. Serves 1.

Spicy Tomato Cocktail

2 cups tomato juice
1 beef flavored bouillon cube
1 teaspoon chopped parsley
2 tablespoons chopped green pepper
1 teaspoon Italian herbs
6 to 8 drops Tabasco sauce
1/4 teaspoon celery salt
1/4 teaspoon onion powder
1/4 teaspoon Worcestershire sauce
1/2 cup sugar-free lemon-lime flavored carbonated beverage

YIELD: 2 1/2 cups
SERVING SIZE: 1/2 cup
PER SERVING: Calories-27
Carbohydrate-5 g.
Protein-1 g.
Fat-trace
Sodium-742 mg.
EXCHANGES: 1 vegetable

Combine all ingredients in blender and whirl. Heat and serve hot in mugs or cold over ice cubes. Serves 5.

Tangy Tomato

1 cup V-8 brand vegetable juice
2 teaspoons lemon juice
1/4 teaspoon Worcestershire sauce
dash of salt

YIELD: 1 cup
SERVING SIZE: 1 cup
PER SERVING: Calories-57
Carbohydrate-12 g.
Protein-1 g.
Fat-trace
Sodium-1015 mg.
EXCHANGES: 2 vegetable

Combine all ingredients and serve over ice. Serves 1.

Strawberry Malt

1/2 cup plain lowfat yogurt
1/4 cup sugar-free strawberry flavored carbonated beverage
1/2 packet Equal brand sweetener
2 tablespoons unsweetened frozen strawberries, slightly thawed

YIELD: 1 cup
SERVING SIZE: 1 cup
PER SERVING: Calories-80
Carbohydrate-9 g.
Protein-6 g.
Fat-2 g.
Sodium-105 mg.
EXCHANGES: 1 skim milk

Whirl all ingredients in blender. Pour into chilled glass. Serves 1.

Grape Malt

1/2 cup plain lowfat yogurt
2 tablespoons unsweetened grape juice concentrate
1/2 packet Equal brand sweetener

YIELD: 1 cup
SERVING SIZE: 1 cup
PER SERVING: Calories-140
Carbohydrate-25 g.
Protein-6 g.
Fat-2 g.
Sodium-81 mg.
EXCHANGES: 1 skim milk, 1 fruit

Whirl all ingredients in blender and serve in chilled glass. Serves 1.

Orange Malt

1/2 cup plain lowfat yogurt
3 tablespoons unsweetened orange juice concentrate
2 tablespoons sugar-free orange flavored carbonated beverage
1/2 packet Equal brand sweetener

YIELD: 1 cup
SERVING SIZE: 1 cup
PER SERVING: Calories-158
Carbohydrate-27 g.
Protein-8 g.
Fat-2 g.
Sodium-88 mg.
EXCHANGES: 1 skim milk, 1 fruit

Whirl yogurt and orange juice concentrate in blender. Add carbonated beverage and sweetener. Whirl again. Serve in chilled glass. Serves 1.

Apple Malt

1/2 cup plain lowfat yogurt
2 tablespoons peeled chopped apple
2 tablespoons unsweetened apple juice concentrate
1/2 packet Equal brand sweetener

YIELD: 1 cup
SERVING SIZE: 1 cup
PER SERVING: Calories-100
Carbohydrate-16 g.
Protein-6 g.
Fat-2 g.
Sodium-82 mg.
EXCHANGES: 1 skim milk

Whirl all ingredients in blender and serve in chilled glass. Serves 1.

Banana Smoothie

1 cup plain lowfat yogurt
1 very ripe banana
1/4 cup unsweetened apple juice
1/4 cup fresh sliced strawberries
3 ice cubes
1 packet Equal brand sweetener

YIELD: 2 cups
SERVING SIZE: 1 cup
PER SERVING: Calories-119
Carbohydrate-21 g.
Protein-4 g.
Fat-2 g.
Sodium-58 mg.
EXCHANGES: 1/2 skim milk, 1 fruit

Whirl all ingredients in blender until smooth. Serves 2.

This can be made ahead and stored in refrigerator for up to one day.

Fruit Yogurt Shake

1 cup plain lowfat yogurt
1/4 teaspoon vanilla
1 packet Equal brand sweetener
3/4 cup frozen unsweetened fruit

YIELD: 2 cups
SERVING SIZE: 1 cup
PER SERVING: Calories-95
Carbohydrate-15 g.
Protein-5 g.
Fat-2 g.
Sodium-63 mg.
EXCHANGES: 1/2 skim milk, 1/2 fruit

Place yogurt, vanilla, and sweetener in blender. Whirl, gradually adding frozen fruit. Serves 2.

Bananas, peaches, blueberries, strawberries, or raspberries work best for this recipe.

Peanut Butter Shake

2 cups cold skim milk
1/3 cup creamy peanut butter
2 tablespoons honey
1 banana, sliced
6 to 8 crushed ice cubes

YIELD: 3 cups
SERVING SIZE: 1/2 cup
PER SERVING: Calories-152
Carbohydrate-17 g.
Protein-7 g.
Fat-7 g.
Sodium-130 mg.
EXCHANGES: 1 skim milk, 1/2 fruit, 1 fat

Place all ingredients except ice cubes in blender. Blend on low speed. Add crushed ice cubes. Blend slowly again until smooth. Serves 6.

Hot Spiced Cider

2 cups unsweetened apple juice
1/2 lemon, sliced thin
1/2 orange, sliced thin
2 cinnamon sticks
2 cups sugar-free ginger ale

YIELD: 4 cups
SERVING SIZE: 1 cup
PER SERVING: Calories-60
Carbohydrate-15 g.
Protein-trace
Fat-trace
Sodium-10 mg.
EXCHANGES: 1 fruit

Combine all ingredients except ginger ale in a saucepan. Cover and simmer for 15 minutes. Add ginger ale and heat 5 minutes more. Remove fruit and cinnamon sticks and serve hot. Serves 4.

Cocoa

1/3 cup nonfat dry milk powder
2 1/2 teaspoons unsweetened cocoa powder
2/3 teaspoon granulated artificial sweetener

YIELD: 6 ounces
SERVING SIZE: 6 ounces
PER SERVING: Calories-93
Carbohydrate-14 g.
Protein-9 g.
Fat-trace
Sodium-124 mg.
EXCHANGES: 1 skim milk

Mix all ingredients thoroughly. To serve, add 3/4 cup hot water. If made in bulk, powder mixture may be stored in plastic bag for later use.

THE JOY OF DIPS AND SPREADS

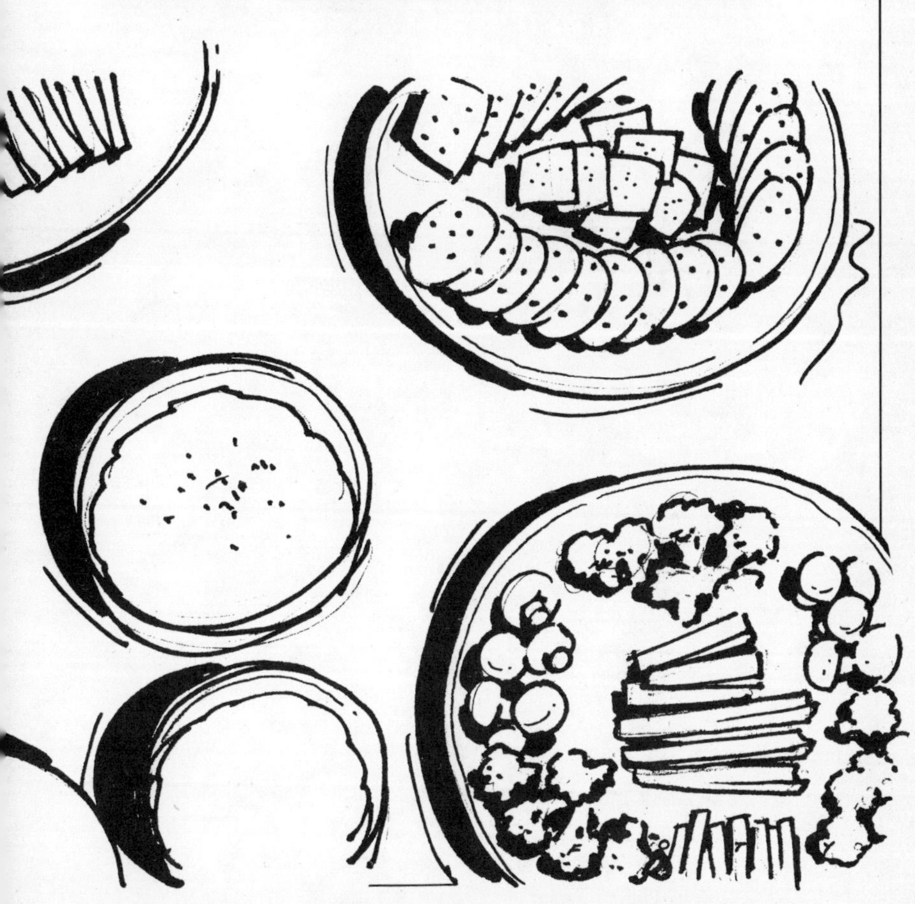

Dips and spreads enhance the flavor of food, but many can be high in fat. The recipes in this section have been modified to reduce fat and calories. Plain lowfat yogurt or lowfat cottage cheese are used in place of sour cream and mayonnaise. Flavorings may be changed according to your personal taste. Experiment with adding your favorite herbs or other seasonings!

Serve these dips with attractive platters of fresh vegetables, crackers, party rye bread, or bite-size pieces of French or sourdough bread.

Curry Vegetable Dip

1/4 cup mayonnaise
3/4 cup plain lowfat yogurt
2 teaspoons tarragon vinegar
1/8 teaspoon thyme
1/2 teaspoon curry powder
2 teaspoons chili sauce

YIELD: 1 cup
SERVING SIZE: 2 tablespoons
PER SERVING: Calories-33
Carbohydrate-1 g.
Protein-4 g.
Fat-3 g.
Sodium-27 mg.
EXCHANGES: 1 fat

Combine all ingredients and chill in refrigerator for at least 3 hours. Serve with crisp raw vegetables.

Skinny Dip

1/2 cup plain lowfat yogurt
1/4 teaspoon dill weed
1 teaspoon minced onion
1/8 teaspoon salt
1/2 packet Equal brand sweetener

YIELD: 1/2 cup
SERVING SIZE: 2 tablespoons
PER SERVING: Calories–18
Carbohydrate–2 g.
Protein–2 g.
Fat–trace
Sodium–91 mg.
EXCHANGES: free

Mix all ingredients thoroughly. Chill several hours. Serve with crisp raw vegetables.

Chili Cheese Dip

1 cup lowfat cottage cheese
3 tablespoons grated Parmesan cheese
1/4 cup chili sauce
1/4 teaspoon onion powder
1/4 cup skim milk

YIELD: 1 1/3 cups
SERVING SIZE: 2 tablespoons
PER SERVING: Calories-33
Carbohydrate-2 g.
Protein-4 g.
Fat-trace
Sodium-190 mg.
EXCHANGES: 1/2 lean meat

Whirl all ingredients in blender until smooth. Chill. Serve with crisp raw vegetables.

Creamy Vegetable Dip

2 tablespoons skim milk
1 12-ounce carton lowfat cottage cheese
1/4 teaspoon garlic powder
dash cayenne
1 teaspoon onion salt
1/4 cup mayonnaise type salad dressing

YIELD: 1 3/4 cups
SERVING SIZE: 2 tablespoons
PER SERVING: Calories-44
Carbohydrate-1 g.
Protein-3 g.
Fat-3 g.
Sodium-219 mg.
EXCHANGES: 1 fat

Whirl all ingredients in a blender one minute or until cheese is smooth. Pour mixture into bowl. Cover and chill. Serve with crisp raw vegetables.

Herb Dip

1/2 cup skim milk
1 cup lowfat cottage cheese
2 tablespoons chopped parsley
2 tablespoons chopped chives
1/2 teaspoon dried basil
1/8 teaspoon curry powder
1/8 teaspoon paprika
1 small garlic clove, minced

YIELD: 1 1/2 cups
SERVING SIZE: 2 tablespoons
PER SERVING: Calories-21
Carbohydrate-1 g.
Protein-3 g.
Fat-trace
Sodium-82 mg.
EXCHANGES: free

Whirl all ingredients in blender until smooth. Serve with crisp raw vegetables.

This is also a delicious sauce served over cooked vegetables.

Nippy Vegetable Dip

1 cup plain lowfat yogurt
1/2 cup chili sauce
1/4 teaspoon celery salt

YIELD: 1 1/2 cups
SERVING SIZE: 2 tablespoons
PER SERVING: Calories-22
Carbohydrate-4 g.
Protein-1 g.
Fat-trace
Sodium-147 mg.
EXCHANGES: free

Stir all ingredients together. Chill. Serve with crisp raw vegetables.

Yogurt Cucumber Vegetable Dip

1/2 cup peeled, shredded cucumber, drained
1 tablespoon minced green onion
1/2 cup plain lowfat yogurt
1/4 teaspoon salt
dash white pepper
1 clove garlic, minced
2 tablespoons finely chopped celery

YIELD: 3/4 cup
SERVING SIZE: 2 tablespoons
PER SERVING: Calories-17
Carbohydrate-3 g.
Protein-1 g.
Fat-trace
Sodium-113 mg.
EXCHANGES: free

Combine all ingredients and carefully blend. Chill 1 to 2 hours. Serve with crisp raw vegetables.

Hawaiian Fruit Spread

1 8-ounce can unsweetened crushed pineapple
1 8-ounce package Neufchâtel cheese, softened
1 teaspoon honey

YIELD: 1 1/2 cups
SERVING SIZE: 2 tablespoons
PER SERVING: Calories-73
Carbohydrate-6 g.
Protein-2 g.
Fat-5 g.
Sodium-82 mg.
EXCHANGES: 1/2 fruit, 1 fat

Thoroughly drain crushed pineapple. Stir together pineapple, cheese, and honey until well blended. Place in a bowl and serve on fresh fruit tray.

Variation: Prepare pineapple-cheese mixture as directed. Stir in 3 tablespoons unsweetened shredded coconut and 2 tablespoons chopped walnuts.

Wonderful with all kinds of fruit!

Peanut Butter Fruit Dip

1/2 cup creamy peanut butter
1/4 cup unsweetened orange juice concentrate, thawed
1/2 cup plain lowfat yogurt

YIELD: 1 1/4 cups
SERVING SIZE: 1 tablespoon
PER SERVING: Calories–37
Carbohydrate–2 g.
Protein–2 g.
Fat–3 g.
Sodium–10 mg.
EXCHANGES: 1 fat

Using electric mixer, beat together all ingredients until fluffy. Cover; chill. Serve with assorted fresh fruits.

Strawberry Spread

1 teaspoon unflavored gelatin
1/2 cup unsweetened orange juice
2 cups mashed or pureed fresh strawberries or 2 cups frozen unsweetened strawberries, thawed and drained
12 packets Equal brand sweetener
2 tablespoons thin orange rind strips

YIELD: 2 1/2 cups
SERVING SIZE: 2 tablespoons
PER SERVING: Calories-12
Carbohydrate-2 g.
Protein-trace
Fat-trace
Sodium-trace
EXCHANGES: free

In small saucepan, sprinkle gelatin over orange juice. Let stand 1 minute. Heat over low heat until gelatin is dissolved and mixture comes to a boil. Remove from heat and add strawberries. Add remaining ingredients and stir to blend. Refrigerate until firm, 3 to 4 hours. Best when used within 1 week.

Fruit Kabobs and Dip

12 fresh strawberries
12 unsweetened, canned pineapple chunks
12 honeydew melon balls

Dip:
1/2 cup fresh strawberries
1/2 cup plain lowfat yogurt
1 teaspoon honey

YIELD: 6 kabobs, 3/4 cup dip
SERVING SIZE: 1 kabob, 2 tablespoons dip
PER SERVING: Calories-38
Carbohydrate-8 g.
Protein-2 g.
Fat-1 g.
Sodium-23 mg.
EXCHANGES: 1/2 fruit

Place fruit on cocktail swords or toothpicks, alternating 2 strawberries, 2 pineapple chunks, and 2 melon balls on each. To prepare dip, whirl all ingredients in blender until smooth.

Salmon and Cucumber Spread

1 cup water packed salmon, drained
1/2 cup finely chopped cucumbers
2 tablespoons chopped green onions
2 tablespoons lemon juice
1/8 teaspoon cayenne pepper
1 tablespoon mayonnaise
1 tablespoon plain lowfat yogurt

YIELD: 1 1/3 cups
SERVING SIZE: 2 tablespoons spread on 2 slices of party rye
PER SERVING: Calories-100
Carbohydrate-8 g.
Protein- 8 g.
Fat-4 g.
Sodium-138 mg.
EXCHANGES: 1 lean meat, 1/2 starch/bread

Combine salmon, cucumber, green onion, lemon juice, and cayenne. Mix mayonnaise and lowfat yogurt. Add to salmon mixture and mix to spreading consistency. Spread on party rye bread.

Dilly Salmon Spread

3 3/4 ounces water packed salmon, drained and flaked
3 ounces Neufchâtel cheese
1/4 cup plain lowfat yogurt
2 tablespoons chopped chives
3 drops of Liquid Smoke
1 teaspoon dried dillweed
1 teaspoon vinegar
1/4 teaspoon salt
pinch of freshly ground pepper

YIELD: 1 cup
SERVING SIZE: 2 tablespoons
PER SERVING: Calories-54
Carbohydrate-2 g.
Protein-4 g.
Fat-4 g.
Sodium-184 mg.
EXCHANGES: 1 fat

Blend salmon and cheese together in a small bowl. Stir in yogurt, chives, Liquid Smoke, dill, vinegar, salt, and pepper. Mix thoroughly. Spread on crackers or use as a dip with vegetables. (Note: To lower sodium content, omit salt.)

Terrific Tuna Dip

1 6 1/2-ounce can water packed tuna
1/2 cup plain lowfat yogurt
1/4 cup reduced calorie mayonnaise
2 tablespoons chopped parsley
2 teaspoons minced onion
2 teaspoons lemon juice
dash white pepper
1/4 teaspoon Worcestershire sauce

YIELD: 1 1/4 cups
SERVING SIZE: 1/4 cup
PER SERVING: Calories-50
Carbohydrate-3 g.
Protein-5 g.
Fat-2 g.
Sodium-84 mg.
EXCHANGES: 1 lean meat

Thoroughly drain tuna and flake with fork. Combine all ingredients except tuna and mix until blended. Add tuna and mix well. Serve on toast, crackers, or raw vegetables.

Spinach Dip

2 cups fresh spinach or 1 10-ounce package frozen chopped spinach
1 bunch green onions, chopped
1 8-ounce can water chestnuts, sliced
1 package Knorr Vegetable Soup Mix
2 tablespoons mayonnaise
1 1/4 cup plain lowfat yogurt
shredded carrots
1 round loaf rye, pumpernickel, or sourdough bread

YIELD: 3 1/2 cups
SERVING SIZE: 4 tablespoons
PER SERVING: Calories-40
Carbohydrate-4 g.
Protein-2 g.
Fat-3 g.
Sodium-163 mg.
EXCHANGES: 1 vegetable, 1/2 fat

If using frozen spinach, thaw and squeeze out water. Combine all ingredients and chill in refrigerator for at least 3 hours before serving. Shredded carrot can be added for more color. Serve in a hollowed out loaf of bread. Use bread cubes for dipping.

THE JOY OF HEARTY SNACKS

Sometimes we need a substantial snack to sooth an especially aggressive appetite. These hearty snacks will do the trick, and can even be used as small meals by themselves. A warm bowl of soup will take the chill off a cold winter afternoon; a slice of pizza will ease late night hunger. All of these recipes are prepared using ingredients lower in fat than traditional recipes.

Crescent Hamburger Roll-ups

1 8-ounce can refrigerated crescent dinner rolls
prepared mustard
1/2 cup cooked lean ground beef (about 4 ounces raw), seasoned with ground pepper and chopped onion
1/2 cup shredded part skim mozzarella cheese

YIELD: 8
SERVING SIZE: 1
PER SERVING: Calories-123
Carbohydrate-14 g.
Protein-7 g.
Fat-4 g.
Sodium-432 mg.
EXCHANGES: 1 starch/bread,
1 medium-fat meat

Unroll crescent dough on baking sheet. Separate dough into 4 squares (2 triangles per square). With fingers, spread out dough to slightly enlarge square. Spread 1/2 to 1 teaspoon mustard on each square. Sprinkle 2 tablespoons cooked ground beef and 2 tablespoons cheese on each square. Roll up dough the long way, making 4 long rolls. Bake at 375° for 10 to 12 minutes. Cut in half. Serve immediately.

'Hole in One' Beef Sandwich

1 hamburger bun, unsliced
3 tablespoons cooked lean ground beef, seasoned with ground pepper and chopped onions
1 tablespoon catsup
1 tablespoon plain lowfat yogurt
1 tablespoon shredded part skim mozzarella cheese

YIELD: 1
SERVING SIZE: 1
PER SERVING: Calories-194
Carbohydrate-25 g.
Protein-18 g.
Fat-4 g.
Sodium-466 mg.
EXCHANGES: 1 1/2 starch/bread, 2 lean meat

Measure a 1 1/2 inch circle on top of bun. Scoop out hole in center of bun and warm bun in oven. Combine cooked ground beef, catsup, yogurt, and 1/2 tablespoon cheese. Stuff in hamburger bun. Top with remaining cheese. Toast in oven at 325° for 10 to 12 minutes, or until heated through.

A Slice of Pizza

1 8-ounce can refrigerated crescent dinner rolls
1/4 cup pizza sauce
3/4 cup cooked lean ground beef, seasoned with ground pepper and chopped onion
1/2 cup shredded part skim mozzarella cheese

YIELD: 8
SERVING SIZE: 1
PER SERVING: Calories-135
Carbohydrate-14 g.
Protein-10 g.
Fat-4 g.
Sodium-455 mg.
EXCHANGES: 1 starch/bread, 1 medium-fat meat

Separate refrigerated dough into 8 triangles; place each flat on baking sheet. Press dough out with fingers to make each triangle slightly larger. Spread each triangle with 1 1/2 teaspoons pizza sauce, 1 1/2 tablespoons cooked seasoned ground beef, and 1 tablespoon cheese. Bake at 375° for 10 to 12 minutes. Serve immediately.

Easy Pizza

1 English muffin, split and toasted
4 teaspoons pizza sauce
3 tablespoons cooked lean ground beef, seasoned with ground pepper and onion
3 tablespoons shredded part skim mozzarella cheese

YIELD: 2
SERVING SIZE: 1
PER SERVING: Calories–128
Carbohydrate–14 g.
Protein–9 g.
Fat–3 g.
Sodium–295 mg.
EXCHANGES: 1 starch/bread, 1 lean meat

Spread each muffin with 2 teaspoons pizza sauce, 1 1/2 tablespoons cooked ground beef, and 1 1/2 tablespoons cheese. Broil until cheese melts. Serve immediately.

Pizza Saucers

1 English muffin, split and toasted
1 tablespoon peanut butter
4 teaspoons pizza sauce
2 tablespoons chopped, cooked ham
3 tablespoons shredded part skim mozzarella cheese

YIELD: 2
SERVING SIZE: 1
PER SERVING: Calories-202
Carbohydrate-16 g.
Protein-9g.
Fat-10 g.
Sodium-314 mg.
EXCHANGES: 1 starch/bread, 1 medium-fat meat, 1 fat

Spread each muffin half with 1/2 tablespoon of peanut butter and 2 teaspoons of pizza sauce. Layer on 1 tablespoon chopped ham and 1 1/2 tablespoons cheese. Broil just until cheese melts. Serve immediately.

Tostada Saucer

1 tostada shell
2 teaspoons light cream cheese
1/4 cup cooked lean ground beef, seasoned with ground pepper and chopped onion
2 tablespoons shredded part skim mozzarella cheese

YIELD: 1
SERVING SIZE: 1
PER SERVING: Calories–219
Carbohydrate–9 g.
Protein–22 g.
Fat–11 g.
Sodium–255 mg.
EXCHANGES: 1/2 starch/bread, 3 lean meat

Heat tostada shell in oven. Spread cream cheese on top of shell. Sprinkle on seasoned cooked ground beef. Top with cheese. Broil just until cheese melts. (If desired, add chopped lettuce, 1/2 chopped tomato, and 1 teaspoon taco sauce.)

Chilled Cucumber Soup

1 cup chicken broth
2 1/2 cups peeled, chopped cucumbers
2 1/2 tablespoons lemon juice
1/2 to 1 teaspoon Worcestershire sauce
dash white pepper
1 teaspoon salt
1 cup plain lowfat yogurt

YIELD: 4 cups
SERVING SIZE: 1 cup
PER SERVING: Calories–54
Carbohydrate–6 g.
Protein–5 g.
Fat–1 g.
Sodium–811 mg.
EXCHANGES: 1/2 milk or 1/2 starch/bread

Combine all ingredients except yogurt in blender. Whirl for 30 seconds or until smooth. Add yogurt and whirl again. Chill thoroughly before serving. Garnish with fresh snipped parsley or thin slice of cucumber. (Note: To reduce sodium content, eliminate salt.)

Low in calories, high in appeal. The coldest thing for a hot summer day!

Seven Vegetable Soup

1 10 3/4-ounce can double strength chicken broth
1/2 cup chopped carrots
1/2 cup chopped celery
1/2 cup chopped onion
1/4 cup finely diced green pepper
1/2 cup finely diced zucchini
1/2 cup chopped mushrooms
1 1/2 cups tomato juice
1/4 teaspoon Worcestershire sauce
1/2 teaspoon Italian herbs

YIELD: 3 1/2 cups
SERVING SIZE: 1 cup
PER SERVING: Calories-48
Carbohydrate-10 g.
Protein-3 g.
Fat-trace
Sodium-351 mg.
EXCHANGES: 2 vegetable

Heat chicken broth and add carrots. Simmer 10 minutes. Add celery, onion, and green pepper; simmer 4 to 5 minutes until celery is tender. Stir in zucchini and mushrooms, simmering until zucchini is soft. Add tomato juice, Worcestershire sauce, and herbs. Simmer until tomato juice is hot, stirring constantly. Serve hot.

A food processor makes this easy. Keep vegetable pieces small.

Easy and Elegant Carrot Soup

1 16-ounce package frozen carrot slices
3 tablespoons instant minced onion
6 to 7 sprigs parsley, chopped
2 tablespoons uncooked rice
4 1/2 cups water
5 chicken-flavored bouillon cubes
1/2 teaspoon sugar
2 teaspoons grated orange rind
1/4 cup orange juice

YIELD: 5 cups
SERVING SIZE: 1 cup
PER SERVING: Calories-82
Carbohydrate-14 g.
Protein-2 g.
Fat-2 g.
Sodium-918 mg.
EXCHANGES: 1 starch/bread

In large skillet, combine carrots, onion, parsley, rice, water, and bouillon cubes. Simmer gently for 20 to 25 minutes until carrots and rice are done. Add sugar and orange rind. Pour into blender and whirl until smooth. Return to skillet. Just before serving, stir in orange juice. Garnish with additional chopped parsley if desired. Serve hot. (Note: To lower sodium content, use low sodium chicken bouillon cubes.)

Keep in refrigerator; heat a cupful in the microwave for a mid-day perker-upper.

Cream of Broccoli Soup

1 8-ounce package frozen chopped broccoli
1 tablespoon instant minced onion
1 cup chicken broth
1 10 3/4-ounce can cream of celery soup
1/4 teaspoon nutmeg, if desired
1 cup plain lowfat yogurt

YIELD: 3 1/2 cups
SERVING SIZE: 1 cup
PER SERVING: Calories-140
Carbohydrate-16 g.
Protein-8 g.
Fat-6 g.
Sodium-984 mg.
EXCHANGES: 1 starch/bread, 1 fat

Cook broccoli as directed on package; drain. In blender, combine broccoli and remaining ingredients except yogurt. Blend until smooth, about 20 seconds. Return to pan and heat, stirring constantly until bubbly. Remove from heat. Stir in yogurt and serve immediately.

79.

THE JOY OF POPCORN TREATS

Everyone loves popcorn, and here are some fun and unusual ways to enjoy it. Have you ever had popcorn with peanut butter and jelly? Or pink perfect popcorn? Here you will even find a lower calorie way to enjoy caramel corn.

For these recipes, pop corn in as little oil as possible or air pop. Popcorn is a good source of carbohydrate and fiber in the diet—truly a healthful and good tasting snack!

Cheesy Barbecue Popcorn

3 tablespoons margarine
1/2 teaspoon chili powder
1/2 teaspoon garlic salt
1/4 teaspoon onion powder
8 cups popped popcorn
1/2 cup grated Parmesan cheese

YIELD: 8 cups
SERVING SIZE: 2 cups
PER SERVING: Calories-180
Carbohydrate-10 g.
Protein-7 g.
Fat-13 g.
Sodium-463 mg.
EXCHANGES: 1/2 starch/bread, 1/2 medium-fat meat, 2 fat

Melt margarine; add seasonings. Pour over air-popped popcorn. Sprinkle cheese over top and mix thoroughly. (Note: To lower sodium content, substitute 1/4 teaspoon garlic powder for the garlic salt.)

Fancy Popcorn Toss

1/4 cup margarine, melted
1/4 teaspoon garlic powder
1/4 teaspoon onion powder
1/4 teaspoon celery salt
2 teaspoons Worcestershire sauce
5 drops Tabasco sauce
6 cups popped popcorn
1 cup chow mein noodles
1 cup pretzel sticks

YIELD: 8 cups
SERVING SIZE: 1 cup
PER SERVING: Calories–240
Carbohydrate–34 g.
Protein–6 g.
Fat–10 g.
Sodium–696 mg.
EXCHANGES: 2 starch/bread, 2 fat

Combine melted margarine with the next 5 ingredients. In large baking pan, mix together popcorn, chow mein noodles, and pretzels. Pour melted margarine and seasonings over popcorn mixture. Stir until well mixed. Bake at 275° for 45 minutes, stirring several times. Serve warm.

Cheese and Onion Popcorn

1/4 cup margarine, melted
1 tablespoon dried onion soup mix
2 cups pretzel sticks
6 cups popped popcorn
1 tablespoon grated Parmesan cheese

YIELD: 8 cups
SERVING SIZE: 1 cup
PER SERVING: Calories–126
Carbohydrate–14 g.
Protein–2 g.
Fat–6 g.
Sodium–214 mg.
EXCHANGES: 1 starch/bread, 1 fat

Stir together melted margarine and onion soup mix. Combine pretzels and popcorn in large baking pan. Pour margarine mixture over pretzels and popcorn, tossing to blend. Sprinkle with Parmesan cheese. Bake at 300° for 10 to 15 minutes, stirring once or twice. Serve warm.

This is so easy. It can be put together right before guests arrive.

84.

Popcorn with Peanut Butter and Jelly

6 cups popped popcorn
1 1/2 tablespoons margarine
1 tablespoon peanut butter
2 teaspoons low-sugar jam spread

YIELD: 6 cups
SERVING SIZE: 1 cup
PER SERVING: Calories-100
Carbohydrate-12 g.
Protein-2 g.
Fat-4 g.
Sodium-46 mg.
EXCHANGES: 1 starch/bread, 1 fat

Keep popcorn warm in oven. Melt margarine over low heat; stir in peanut butter and jam spread, blending thoroughly. Pour over warm popcorn, quickly stirring to coat all pieces.

Pink Perfect Popcorn

6 cups popped popcorn
2 1/2 tablespoons margarine
1 teaspoon sugar-free strawberry flavored gelatin

YIELD: 6 cups
SERVING SIZE: 1 cup
PER SERVING: Calories-112
Carbohydrate-14 g.
Protein-2 g.
Fat-6 g.
Sodium-80 mg.
EXCHANGES: 1 starch/bread, 1 fat

Keep popcorn warm in oven. In small saucepan over low heat, melt margarine. Cool slightly. Quickly stir in strawberry gelatin and immediately pour over popcorn tossing to coat all pieces.

Caramel Popcorn

6 cups popped popcorn
2 tablespoons margarine
2 tablespoons honey

YIELD: 6 cups
SERVING SIZE: 1 cup
PER SERVING: Calories-108
Carbohydrate-16 g.
Protein-2 g.
Fat-4 g.
Sodium-42 mg.
EXCHANGES: 1 starch/bread, 1 fat

Spread popcorn evenly in large shallow baking pan. In small saucepan, melt margarine and blend in honey. Pour over popcorn, stirring to coat all pieces. Bake at 325° for 8 to 10 minutes, stirring often. Cool slightly in pan before removing. Store in airtight container.

Chocolate Popcorn

6 cups popped popcorn
1 tablespoon margarine
2 tablespoons light corn syrup
1 tablespoon cocoa powder
1 1/2 tablespoons skim milk
1/8 teaspoon salt

YIELD: 6 cups
SERVING SIZE: 1 cup
PER SERVING: Calories–94
Carbohydrate–16 g.
Protein–2 g.
Fat–2 g.
Sodium–82 mg.
EXCHANGES: 1 starch/bread

Keep popcorn warm in oven while making chocolate sauce. In small pan, melt margarine over low heat. Add corn syrup, cocoa, milk, and salt. Stir over low heat until well blended and mixture is hot. Pour over warm popcorn. Quickly stir to coat all pieces.

Popcorn Balls

5 cups popped popcorn
1/4 cup honey
1/4 cup creamy peanut butter

YIELD: 9
SERVING SIZE: 1
PER SERVING: Calories–98
Carbohydrate–14 g.
Protein–3 g.
Fat–4 g.
Sodium–35 mg.
EXCHANGES: 1 starch/bread, 1 fat

Put popcorn in large pan. Keep popcorn warm in 250° oven. (Popcorn must be warm when hot honey mixture is added.) In small pan over medium heat boil honey for 1 to 2 minutes. Reduce heat and quickly add peanut butter; stir until well blended. Remove popcorn from oven and immediately drizzle honey mixture over popcorn, constantly stirring to coat evenly. Tear off 9 sheets of waxed paper approximately 10 x 10 inches. Place a little more than a half cup of popcorn in center of waxed paper square. Fold corners of paper up around popcorn and twist top, pressing popcorn to make a ball. Continue for remaining popcorn. Store in airtight container.

ESPECIALLY FOR KIDS

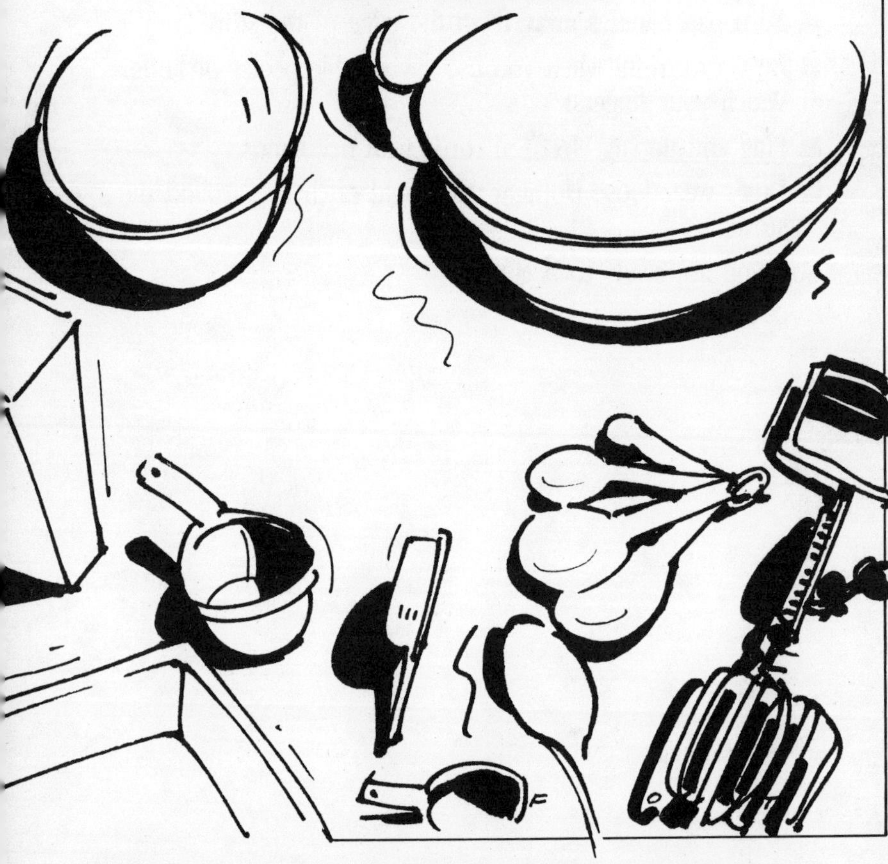

Cooking is fun! You can share the fun when you make these recipes for your friends and family. Here are a few rules to remember:

- Before you start, make sure it's okay for you to use the kitchen.
- Always wash your hands.
- Read the recipe all the way through before starting.
- Make sure you have all the ingredients and utensils you need.

- Wipe up spills right away.
- Always use potholders when you touch a hot pan or pot.
- Turn pan handles away from the edge of the stove.
- Be very careful when you use a vegetable peeler or knife. Watch your fingers!
- Plug and unplug electrical cords with dry hands.
- Don't wear loose clothing that could catch fire around the stove.

Now you are ready to begin!

91.

After School Pizza Spinner

WHAT YOU NEED:

1 7 1/2 ounce can refrigerator biscuits
1/2 cup pizza sauce
2/3 cup chopped, cooked ham
2/3 cup shredded part skim mozzarella cheese

WHAT YOU DO:

1. On baking sheet, flatten out each biscuit with fingers until doubled in size.
2. Spread 2 teaspoons pizza sauce on each biscuit.
3. Sprinkle 1 tablespoon ham over sauce; top with 1 tablespoon cheese.
4. Bake at 400° for 8 to 10 minutes.

Variation: Substitute 2/3 cup cooked lean ground beef seasoned with ground pepper for ham. Bake as directed.

YIELD: 10
SERVING SIZE: 1
PER SERVING: Calories-102
Carbohydrate-11 g.
Protein-6 g.
Fat-3 g.
Sodium-294 mg.
EXCHANGES: 1 starch/bread, 1/2 medium-fat meat

Tasty Tuna Sailboats

WHAT YOU NEED:

1 6 1/2-ounce can water-packed tuna
2 tablespoons finely chopped celery
2 tablespoons reduced calorie mayonnaise
2 teaspoons finely chopped onion
1 teaspoon lemon juice
4 hamburger buns, unsliced

WHAT YOU DO:

1. Drain tuna; flake into medium sized bowl.
2. Stir in all remaining ingredients except hamburger buns.
3. Scoop out center of each hamburger bun.
4. Stuff each bun with 1/4 cup of tuna mixture.
5. Put stalk of celery with leaves in each bun to make a sailboat.
6. Enjoy.

YIELD: 4 sandwiches
SERVING SIZE: 1 sandwich
PER SERVING: Calories-175
Carbohydrate-21 g.
Protein-15 g.
Fat-4 g.
Sodium-440 mg.
EXCHANGES: 1 1/2 starch/bread, 1 1/2 lean meat

93.

Classy Chicken-Cheese Sandwiches

WHAT YOU NEED:

3 tablespoons diced, cooked chicken
2 teaspoons mayonnaise
1 to 2 chopped dill pickles, if desired
1 tablespoon shredded part skim mozzarella cheese
2 slices bread
2 lettuce leaves

WHAT YOU DO:

1. Mix together diced chicken, mayonnaise, pickles, and cheese.
2. Spread on 1 slice of bread.
3. Top with lettuce.
4. Add other slice of bread.

Variation: Substitute 2 tablespoons unsweetened crushed pineapple, drained, and 1 tablespoon chopped celery for dill pickle and cheese.

YIELD: 1 sandwich
SERVING SIZE: 1 sandwich
PER SERVING: Calories-248
Carbohydrate-29 g.
Protein-18 g.
Fat-8 g.
Sodium-3255 mg. if made with pickles; 400 mg. if made without pickle
EXCHANGES: 2 starch/bread, 2 lean meat

A good way to use mom's leftover chicken.

Sandwich Specials I

WHAT YOU NEED:
2 slices bread
1 1/2 tablespoons peanut butter
1/2 banana, sliced

WHAT YOU DO:
1. Spread peanut butter on 1 slice of bread.
2. Put banana slices on top of peanut butter. Top with other slice of bread.

YIELD: 1 sandwich
SERVING SIZE: 1/2 sandwich
PER SERVING: Calories-158
Carbohydrate-20 g.
Protein-6 g.
Fat-7 g.
Sodium-185 mg.
EXCHANGES: 1 starch/bread, 1/2 fruit, 1/2 high-fat meat, 1/2 fat

Peanut butter stick-to-the-roof-of-your-mouth sandwich!

Sandwich Specials II

WHAT YOU NEED:
2 slices bread
1 1/2 tablespoons peanut butter
2 tablespoons chopped apple

WHAT YOU DO:
1. Spread peanut butter on 1 slice of bread.
2. Put apple slices on top of peanut butter. Top with other slice of bread.

YIELD: 1 sandwich
SERVING SIZE: 1/2 sandwich
PER SERVING: Calories-147
Carbohydrate-16 g.
Protein-5 g.
Fat-7 g.
Sodium-185 mg.
EXCHANGES: 1 starch/bread, 1/2 high-fat meat, 1/2 fat

Sandwich Specials III

WHAT YOU NEED:
2 slices bread
1 1/2 tablespoons peanut butter
1 1/2 tablespoons raisins, chopped

WHAT YOU DO:
1. Spread peanut butter on 1 slice of bread.
2. Put raisins on top of peanut butter. Top with other slice of bread.

YIELD: 1 sandwich
SERVING SIZE: 1/2 sandwich
PER SERVING: Calories-151
Carbohydrate-17 g.
Protein-5 g.
Fat-7 g.
Sodium-185 mg.
EXCHANGES: 1 starch/bread, 1/2 high-fat meat, 1/2 fat

Noisy Celery Canoes

WHAT YOU NEED:
2 stalks celery
1 hard cooked egg
1 1/2 teaspoons reduced calorie mayonnaise
dash of salt
1/4 teaspoon prepared mustard, if desired
1 1/2 teaspoons shredded cheddar cheese

WHAT YOU DO:
1. Wash and trim celery.
2. Peel hard cooked egg; chop up.
3. Add mayonnaise, salt, mustard, and cheese to egg.
4. Spread egg filling in celery.

YIELD: 2 canoes
SERVING SIZE: 2 canoes
PER SERVING: Calories-140
Carbohydrate-6 g.
Protein-8 g.
Fat-10 g.
Sodium-576 mg.
EXCHANGES: 1 vegetable, 1 medium-fat meat, 1 fat

Lettuce Roll-ups

WHAT YOU NEED:
3 large lettuce leaves
1 tablespoon light cream cheese
1 tablespoon sunflower seeds, sesame seeds, or wheat germ
toothpicks

WHAT YOU DO:
1. Wash lettuce leaves.
2. Spread 1 teaspoon cheese on each lettuce leaf.
3. Sprinkle with seeds or wheat germ.
4. Roll up.
5. Fasten with toothpick.

YIELD: 3 lettuce leaves
SERVING SIZE: 3 lettuce leaves
PER SERVING: Calories-156
Carbohydrate-3 g.
Protein-6 g.
Fat-13 g.
Sodium-119 mg.
EXCHANGES: 1 high-fat meat, 1 fat

Peanut Yogurt Swirls

WHAT YOU NEED:
2 teaspoons peanut butter
2 graham cracker squares
1 tablespoon plain lowfat yogurt
nutmeg
cinnamon

WHAT YOU DO:
1. Spread 1 teaspoon peanut butter on each graham cracker square.
2. Spread 1/2 tablespoon yogurt on top of peanut butter.
3. Sprinkle with nutmeg and cinnamon.

YIELD: 2 squares
SERVING SIZE: 2 squares
PER SERVING: Calories-125
Carbohydrate-13 g.
Protein-4 g.
Fat-7 g.
Sodium-167 mg.
EXCHANGES: 1 starch/bread, 1 fat

Cheese and Cracker Dunk

WHAT YOU NEED:
1/2 teaspoon margarine
1 tablespoon grated cheddar cheese
4 single soda crackers

WHAT YOU DO:
1. In small skillet, melt together margarine and cheese over very low heat.
2. When melted, turn off heat.
3. Dunk 2 sides of crackers in cheese dip. Use opposite corner of crackers as a "handle."
4. Enjoy

YIELD: 4 crackers
SERVING SIZE: 4 crackers
PER SERVING: Calories-97
Carbohydrate-9 g.
Protein-1 g.
Fat-5 g.
Sodium-225 mg.
EXCHANGES: 1/2 starch/bread, 1 fat

After School Energy Dip

WHAT YOU NEED:
1/3 cup lowfat cottage cheese
2 tablespoons grated cheddar cheese
1/4 teaspoon dill weed
1/8 teaspoon salt
1/4 teaspoon onion powder
prepared vegetable sticks (carrots, celery)

WHAT YOU DO:

1. Mash cottage cheese with fork.
2. Add remaining ingredients except vegetables.
3. Stir together until well blended.
4. Use as dip for fresh vegetables.

YIELD: 1/2 cup
SERVING SIZE: 2 tablespoons
PER SERVING: Calories-75
Carbohydrate-1 g.
Protein-6 g.
Fat-5 g.
Sodium-211 mg.
EXCHANGES: 1 medium-fat meat

GORP Trail Mix*

WHAT YOU NEED:
1 cup Bran Chex cereal
1 cup Wheat Chex cereal
1 cup Corn Chex cereal
1 cup salted sunflower seeds
1 cup salted peanuts
1 cup raisins
1 cup unsweetened shredded coconut

WHAT YOU DO:
1. Mix all ingredients together.
2. Store in an airtight container.

YIELD: 7 cups
SERVING SIZE: 1/3 cup
PER SERVING: Calories-116
Carbohydrate-12 g.
Protein-4 g.
Fat-6 g.
Sodium-110 mg.
EXCHANGES: 1 starch/bread, 1 fat

**Good Ol' Raisins and Peanuts*

Homemade Trail Mix

WHAT YOU NEED:

3 tablespoons raisins
2 tablespoons peanuts
2 tablespoons sunflower seeds
2 tablespoons unsweetened shredded coconut
1 tablespoon semisweet mini chocolate chips

WHAT YOU DO:

1. Mix all ingredients together.
2. Store in airtight container.

YIELD: 10 tablespoons
SERVING SIZE: 5 tablespoons
PER SERVING: Calories-187
Carbohydrate-18 g.
Protein-5 g.
Fat-12 g.
Sodium-55 mg.
EXCHANGES: 1 starch/bread, 2 fat

104.

Chocolate Arrows I

WHAT YOU NEED:
1 teaspoon margarine
1 tablespoon mini semisweet chocolate chips
32 pretzel sticks

WHAT YOU DO:
1. Melt margarine and chocolate chips together in a small pan over low heat, stirring constantly.
2. Remove from heat when melted.
3. Dunk end of each pretzel stick in chocolate.
4. Put on rack to cool.

YIELD: 32 arrows
SERVING SIZE: 8 arrows
PER SERVING: Calories-84
Carbohydrate-9 g.
Protein-1 g.
Fat-5 g.
Sodium-176 mg.
EXCHANGES: 1/2 starch/bread, 1 fat

This recipe makes a lot, so call in your friends.

Chocolate Arrows II

WHAT YOU NEED:

1 teaspoon margarine
1 tablespoon mini semisweet chocolate chips
2 apples, cut into 16 slices each

WHAT YOU DO:

1. Melt margarine and chocolate chips together in a small pan over low heat, stirring constantly.
2. Remove from heat when melted.
3. Dunk end of each apple slice in chocolate.
4. Put on rack to cool.

YIELD: 32 arrows
SERVING SIZE: 8 arrows
PER SERVING: Calories-79
Carbohydrate-10 g.
Protein-1 g.
Fat-5 g.
Sodium-11 mg.
EXCHANGES: 1/2 fruit, 1 fat

Chocolate Arrows III

WHAT YOU NEED:

1 teaspoon margarine
1 tablespoon mini semisweet chocolate chips
32 pretzel sticks
2 bananas

WHAT YOU DO:

1. Melt margarine and chocolate chips together in a small pan over low heat, stirring constantly.
2. Remove from heat when melted.
3. Cut each banana in half lengthwise. Cut each half into 8 slices.
4. "Spear" each banana slice with a pretzel stick.
5. Dunk each banana slice in chocolate.
6. Put on rack to cool.

YIELD: 32 arrows
SERVING SIZE: 8 arrows
PER SERVING: Calories-136
Carbohydrate-23 g.
Protein-2 g.
Fat-5 g.
Sodium-176 mg.
EXCHANGES: 1 fruit, 1/2 starch/bread, 1 fat

107.

Secret Sunflower Banana Bread

WHAT YOU NEED:

3 medium ripe bananas
1/4 cup margarine, melted
1/4 cup honey
1 tablespoon unsweetened orange juice concentrate
1 1/2 cups whole wheat flour
1 teaspoon baking soda
1/4 teaspoon salt
1 teaspoon vanilla
1/2 cup sunflower seeds

WHAT YOU DO:

1. Peel bananas; put in medium-sized bowl and mash with fork.
2. Stir in melted margarine, honey, and orange juice concentrate.
3. In separate bowl, stir together flour, soda, and salt; add to bananas.
4. Add vanilla and sunflower seeds; mix well.
5. Pour into oiled 9 x 5 inch loaf pan.
6. Bake at 350° for 55 to 60 minutes.
7. Remove from pan; cool before slicing.

YIELD: 1 loaf (16 slices)
SERVING SIZE: 1 slice
PER SERVING: Calories-139
Carbohydrate-19 g.
Protein-4 g.
Fat-6 g.
Sodium-87 mg.
EXCHANGES: 1 starch/bread, 1 fat

It's a secret how you can make such yummy banana bread.

Nutty Banana Boats

WHAT YOU NEED:

1 banana

3 teaspoons chunky peanut butter

1 teaspoon wheat germ

2 teaspoons unsweetened shredded coconut

2 teaspoons raisins

WHAT YOU DO:

1. Peel banana and cut in half the long way.
2. Spread 1 1/2 teaspoons of peanut butter on each half.
3. Sprinkle half of wheat germ on each banana half.
4. Sprinkle half of the coconut on each.

YIELD: 2

SERVING SIZE: 1

PER SERVING: Calories-121
Carbohydrate-17 g.
Protein-3 g.
Fat-5 g.
Sodium-38 mg.

EXCHANGES: 1 fruit, 1 fat

Crunchy Apple Treasures

WHAT YOU NEED:

1 medium apple
3 tablespoons peanut butter
3 tablespoons crisp rice cereal

WHAT YOU DO:

1. Cut apple into 8 slices.
2. Combine peanut butter and cereal.
3. Spread mixture on apple slices.

YIELD: 8 slices
SERVING SIZE: 4 slices
PER SERVING: Calories-189
Carbohydrate-14 g.
Protein-6 g.
Fat-12 g.
Sodium-144 mg.
EXCHANGES: 1 fruit, 1 high-fat meat, 1 fat

Apple Cheese Squares

WHAT YOU NEED:

12 graham cracker squares
2 tablespoons light cream cheese
1 apple, cut into 12 slices
2 tablespoons unsweetened shredded coconut

WHAT YOU DO:

1. Spread each graham cracker with 1/2 teaspoon cream cheese.
2. Put 1 apple slice on top and sprinkle with 1/2 teaspoon coconut.
3. Enjoy!

YIELD: 12 crackers
SERVING SIZE: 2 crackers
PER SERVING: Calories-95
Carbohydrate-15 g.
Protein-2 g.
Fat-3 g.
Sodium-79 mg.
EXCHANGES: 1 starch/bread, 1/2 fat

Fizzy Fruit Cup

WHAT YOU NEED:
1/2 cup chopped orange
1/2 cup sliced bananas
1/2 cup chopped apples
1/2 cup sliced strawberries
2 tablespoons raisins
1 12-ounce can sugar-free lemon-lime flavored carbonated beverage

WHAT YOU DO:
1. Mix fruits and raisins in a bowl.
2. Spoon into 4 paper cups.
3. Pour soda over fruit. Eat with a spoon!

YIELD: 4 cups
SERVING SIZE: 1 cup
PER SERVING: Calories-82
Carbohydrate-20 g.
Protein-1 g.
Fat-trace
Sodium-21 mg.
EXCHANGES: 1 1/2 fruit

Purple Ice

WHAT YOU NEED:
3/4 cup unsweetened grape juice
1/2 cup vanilla ice milk
3/4 cup plain lowfat yogurt

WHAT YOU DO:
1. Combine all ingredients in blender.
2. Blend until smooth.
3. Pour over ice into 2 glasses.

YIELD: 2 cups
SERVING SIZE: 1 cup
PER SERVING: Calories-136
Carbohydrate-25 g.
Protein-5 g.
Fat-2 g.
Sodium-86 mg.
EXCHANGES: 1 fruit, 1 skim milk or 1 fruit, 1 starch/bread

Fruit Knox Blox

WHAT YOU NEED:
4 envelopes unflavored gelatin
3 envelopes any fruit flavored sugar-free gelatin
4 cups boiling water

WHAT YOU DO:
1. In large bowl, mix unflavored gelatin with fruit flavored gelatin.
2. Add boiling water and stir until dissolved.
3. Pour into 9 x 13 inch pan.
4. Chill until firm.
5. To serve, cut into 9 rows of 12 squares each.

YIELD: 108 squares
SERVING SIZE: 12 squares
PER SERVING: Calories-21
Carbohydrate-trace
Protein-3 g.
Fat-trace
Sodium-trace
EXCHANGES: free

Great finger food!

Cranberry Grape Cubes

WHAT YOU NEED:

4 envelopes unflavored gelatin

4 cups reduced calorie cranberry juice (other fruit juices may be used, except for fresh or frozen pineapple juice)

WHAT YOU DO:

1. In large saucepan, sprinkle unflavored gelatin over juice; let stand one minute.
2. Stir over low heat until gelatin is completely dissolved.
3. Pour into 9 x 13 inch pan.
4. Chill until firm.
5. To serve, cut into nine rows of 12 squares each.

YIELD: 108 squares
SERVING SIZE: 6 squares
PER SERVING: Calories-38
Carbohydrate-8 g.
Protein-1 g.
Fat-trace
Sodium-trace
EXCHANGES: 1/2 fruit

Orange Julius

WHAT YOU NEED:

1 6-ounce can unsweetened orange juice concentrate
2/3 cup skim milk
2/3 cup water
1 teaspoon vanilla
8 ice cubes
2 packets Equal brand sweetener

WHAT YOU DO:

1. Put all ingredients in a blender.
2. Blend until thick, about 1 minute.
3. Pour into 3 glasses.

YIELD: 2 cups
SERVING SIZE: 2/3 cup
PER SERVING: Calories-78
Carbohydrate-16 g.
Protein-3 g.
Fat-trace
Sodium-29 mg.
EXCHANGES: 1 fruit

Triple Treat Cooler

WHAT YOU NEED:

1 cup unsweetened grape juice
1 12-ounce can sugar-free ginger ale
1 cup unsweetened orange juice

WHAT YOU DO:

1. Put grape juice, ginger ale, and orange juice in a pitcher and mix.
2. Put ice cubes in 4 tall glasses.
3. Pour mixture into glasses and enjoy.

YIELD: 3 1/2 cups
SERVING SIZE: 3/4 cup
PER SERVING: Calories-66
Carbohydrate-16 g.
Protein-trace
Fat-trace
Sodium-21 mg.
EXCHANGES: 1 fruit

Refreshing Orangeade

WHAT YOU NEED:

2 cups unsweetened orange juice
1 cup unsweetened pineapple juice
1 tablespoon lemon juice
1 packet Equal brand sweetener
5 ice cubes

WHAT YOU DO:

1. Put all ingredients into blender.
2. Blend for 3 seconds.
3. Pour into 4 tall glasses.

YIELD: 3 cups
SERVING SIZE: 3/4 cup
PER SERVING: Calories-92
Carbohydrate-21 g.
Protein-1 g.
Fat-trace
Sodium-trace
EXCHANGES: 1 1/2 fruit

119.
THE JOY OF

RISE 'N SHINE BREAKFASTS

Begin each morning with a nutrition-packed breakfast and you'll start your day off right! Many of these recipes make perfect take-along snacks for mornings on the run. You will also find pancakes and French toast with a new twist, filling breakfast drinks, and alternatives to sweet rolls and doughnuts.

These recipes use tasty ingredients that increase complex carbohydrates and fiber and reduce fat and sugar. Stock your kitchen with cereals, oats, dried fruits, and plain lowfat yogurt and you'll be ready for a nutritious breakfast.

Breakfast Nog

1 egg
1/2 cup plain lowfat yogurt
2 packets Equal brand sweetener
1/2 teaspoon vanilla
1 tablespoon peanut butter

YIELD: 1 cup
SERVING SIZE: 1/2 cup
PER SERVING: Calories-127
Carbohydrate-6 g.
Protein-8 g.
Fat-8 g.
Sodium-112 mg.
EXCHANGES: 1/2 skim milk, 1/2 medium-fat meat, 1 fat

Whirl all ingredients in blender until smooth. Serve immediately. Serves 2.

Instant Breakfast

1 cup unsweetened orange juice
1 small carrot, cut into chunks
1 small banana
1 egg
2 tablespoons nonfat dry milk powder
1 teaspoon honey

YIELD: 1 2/3 cups
SERVING SIZE: 3/4 cup
PER SERVING: Calories-190
Carbohydrate-35 g.
Protein-6 g.
Fat-3 g.
Sodium-93 mg.
EXCHANGES: 2 fruit, 1/2 skim milk, 1/2 fat

Whirl all ingredients in blender for a few seconds. Serve immediately. Serves 2.

This is not only good—it's delicious and nutritious.

Homemade Granola

4 cups quick-cooking rolled oats
1/2 cup Grape-Nuts cereal
granulated sugar substitute equal to 1/4 cup sugar
1 cup chopped peanuts
1/3 cup oil
1/2 cup wheat germ
1/2 cup raisins

YIELD: 6 1/2 cups
SERVING SIZE: 1/4 cup
PER SERVING: Calories-140
Carbohydrate-15 g.
Protein-5 g.
Fat-7 g.
Sodium-57 mg.
EXCHANGES: 1 starch/bread, 1 fat

Spread oats on a baking sheet and heat at 350° for 10 minutes. Combine remaining ingredients except wheat germ and raisins. Bake on ungreased baking sheet for 20 minutes, stirring once to brown evenly; allow mixture to cool in the oven. Stir in oats, wheat germ, and raisins. Refrigerate in glass jars or plastic containers.

Nutty Fruit Nibbles

1 tablespoon margarine, melted
1/4 cup walnuts, coarsely chopped
1/4 cup raisins
1/4 cup sunflower seeds
1/4 cup unsweetened shredded coconut
1/4 cup unsweetened chopped dates
1/4 cup quick-cooking rolled oats

YIELD: 1 1/2 cups
SERVING SIZE: 1/4 cup
PER SERVING: Calories-162
Carbohydrate-15 g.
Protein-3 g.
Fat-10 g.
Sodium-28 mg.
EXCHANGES: 1 starch/bread, 2 fat

Stir all ingredients together in skillet until heated and thoroughly mixed. Serve warm or cold.

Glazed Granola

2 cups quick-cooking rolled oats
1 cup unsweetened shredded coconut
1/2 cup wheat germ
1/2 cup sunflower seeds
1/4 cup slivered almonds
1/2 cup margarine
1/4 cup honey
1/2 teaspoon salt
2 cups raisins

YIELD: 7 cups
SERVING SIZE: 1/4 cup
PER SERVING: Calories-128
Carbohydrate-16 g.
Protein-3 g.
Fat-7 g.
Sodium-82 mg.
EXCHANGES: 1 starch/bread, 1 fat

In large bowl, combine oats, coconut, wheat germ, sunflower seeds, and almonds. In small saucepan, melt together margarine, honey, and salt. Pour over dry ingredients, mixing well. Spread granola over oiled 15 x 10 inch jelly roll pan. Bake at 350° for 30 minutes or until golden brown, stirring several times. Remove from oven; stir in raisins while still hot. Cool. Store in tightly covered container.

Breakfast Granola Bars

2 large eggs
1/4 teaspoon salt
1/2 teaspoon vanilla
2 1/2 cups glazed granola (see recipe page 125)

YIELD: 12
SERVING SIZE: 1
PER SERVING: Calories-119
Carbohydrate-13 g.
Protein-4 g.
Fat-6 g.
Sodium-59 mg.
EXCHANGES: 1 starch/bread, 1 fat

In medium sized bowl, combine eggs, salt, and vanilla. Whip until well blended. Add granola and mix well. Press into oiled 8 inch square pan. Bake at 350° for 15 to 20 minutes. Cut into 12 bars.

These bars are easy and portable—so quick you can make in the morning and take with you.

Oatmeal Breakfast Bars

1/3 cup margarine
1/2 cup sugar
3 eggs
1/2 cup nonfat dry milk powder
2 tablespoons molasses
2 1/2 teaspoons vanilla
1 package dry Butter Buds brand Natural Butter Flavored Mix
1 cup whole wheat flour
1 cup unprocessed bran
3 cups quick-cooking rolled oats
1 teaspoon baking powder
2 teaspoons cinnamon
1 cup raisins

YIELD: 24
SERVING SIZE: 1
PER SERVING: Calories-130
Carbohydrate-21 g.
Protein-3 g.
Fat-4 g.
Sodium-58 mg.
EXCHANGES: 1 starch/bread, 1 fat

Cream together margarine and sugar. Beat in eggs, milk powder, molasses, and vanilla; add Butter Buds and mix well. Stir in flour, bran, oats, baking powder, cinnamon, and raisins. Mix well. Pat mixture into oiled 9 x 13 inch pan, bake at 350° for 15 minutes. Cool.

Baked Breakfast Fruit

2 eggs
1 tablespoon honey
1 20-ounce can unsweetened pineapple chunks or tidbits, drained, reserving juice
1 16-ounce can unsweetened sliced pears, drained
2 tablespoons margarine
5 slices bread, cubed

YIELD: 10
SERVING SIZE: 1
PER SERVING: Calories-135
Carbohydrate-24 g.
Protein-3 g.
Fat-4 g.
Sodium-180 mg.
EXCHANGES: 1 fruit, 1/2 starch/bread, 1 fat

Beat together eggs and honey. Add reserved pineapple juice and stir well. Spread pineapple chunks over bottom of oiled 8-inch square pan. Cut pear slices into chunks and add to pineapple in pan, stirring to blend. Pour egg mixture over fruit. Melt margarine in skillet; add bread cubes and sauté until cubes are slightly browned. Spread bread cubes evenly over fruit mixture, pressing down slightly. Bake at 350° for 30 minutes. Cut into 10 squares. Serve warm.

The perfect accompaniment to hot cereal on a chilly morning.

129.

Strawberry Surprise French Toast

4 slices French bread cut 1-inch thick
3 tablespoons low-sugar strawberry spread
2 eggs
1/2 cup skim milk
1 tablespoon oil for frying

YIELD: 4
SERVING SIZE: 1
PER SERVING: Calories-160
Carbohydrate-17 g.
Protein-7 g.
Fat-7 g.
Sodium-200 mg.
EXCHANGES: 1 starch/bread,
1 medium-fat meat

Make a pocket in each bread slice by cutting each slice in half lengthwise, almost but not entirely through to the other side. Stuff about 2 teaspoons of strawberry spread in pocket of each bread slice. Place each slice flat in a 9-inch pie pan. In small bowl, beat together eggs and milk and pour evenly over bread slices. Cover and refrigerate at least 1 hour or overnight until most of the liquid is absorbed. When ready to serve, heat oil in a skillet and fry bread slices about 3 minutes on each side until golden brown, turning once. Serve hot.

Great for teenage slumber parties or as a breakfast snack.

Cottage Cheese Pancakes

3 eggs
1 cup lowfat cottage cheese
1 tablespoon oil
2 tablespoons wheat germ
1/4 cup all-purpose flour
2 tablespoons oil, for frying

YIELD: 16 silver dollar-sized pancakes
SERVING SIZE: 2
PER SERVING: Calories-146
Carbohydrate-6 g.
Protein-8 g.
Fat-10 g.
Sodium-140 mg.
EXCHANGES: 1/2 starch/bread, 1 medium-fat meat, 1 fat

Whirl eggs in blender. Add cottage cheese, 1 tablespoon oil, and wheat germ. Whirl again. Add flour and whirl a few seconds more. Fry pancakes on non-stick, oiled griddle or fry pan, using about 1 1/2 tablespoons batter per pancake. Serve hot.

Very unusual and very good! Make the batter the night before and keep in refrigerator.

Baked Oatmeal Breakfast

2/3 cup cooked oatmeal
3/4 cup unsweetened crushed pineapple, undrained
1/2 cup nonfat dry milk powder
1/4 cup raisins
2 tablespoons wheat germ
1/4 teaspoon cinnamon, if desired

YIELD: 6
SERVING SIZE: 1
PER SERVING: Calories-102
Carbohydrate-19 g.
Protein-6 g.
Fat-1 g.
Sodium-55 mg.
EXCHANGES: 1 starch/bread, 1/2 skim milk

Stir all ingredients together until well blended. If mixture seems thick, add 1 or 2 teaspoons water. Spoon into 6 foil-lined muffin cups or oiled custard dishes, allowing about 1/3 cup per serving. Bake at 350° for 15 minutes. Serve hot.

Baked in a muffin cup, this can easily be a take-along breakfast.

Peanut Apple Toasty

1 slice bread, toasted
2 teaspoons peanut butter
1/2 medium apple, thinly sliced
cinnamon
1/2 teaspoon honey
1 teaspoon raisins

YIELD: 1
SERVING SIZE: 1
PER SERVING: Calories-168
Carbohydrate-26 g.
Protein-5 g.
Fat-6 g.
Sodium-142 mg.
EXCHANGES: 1 1/2 starch/bread, 1 fat

Spread peanut butter on toast. Place apple slices on top of peanut butter. Sprinkle with cinnamon and drizzle with honey. Broil 3 minutes. Sprinkle raisins on top. Broil 1 more minute. Serve warm.

Don't limit this just to breakfast. It's good any time of day!

Chocolate Crumb Coffee Cake

2 cups all-purpose flour
1 cup whole wheat flour
1 cup sugar
1/2 cup margarine
2 tablespoons cinnamon
1 tablespoon cocoa powder
1 teaspoon nutmeg
1/4 teaspoon salt
1 cup raisins
1/8 teaspoon ground cloves
2 cups lowfat buttermilk
1 teaspoon baking soda
1/2 teaspoon baking powder

YIELD: 18
SERVING SIZE: 1
PER SERVING: Calories–200
Carbohydrate–35 g.
Protein–4 g.
Fat–5 g.
Sodium–185 mg.
EXCHANGES: 2 starch/bread, 1 fat

In a bowl, combine flours and sugar; cut in margarine until crumbly. Set aside 1 cup of the mixture to use as a topping. To remaining mixture, add cinnamon, cocoa, nutmeg, salt, raisins, and cloves. Mix buttermilk, soda, and baking powder, then add to flour-spice mixture. Pour into oiled and floured 9 x 13 inch pan. Sprinkle on reserved topping and bake at 325° for 30 to 35 minutes or until done. Cut into 18 squares.

Easy Cinnamon Rolls

1 loaf frozen bread dough
1/4 cup margarine, softened
2 tablespoons cinnamon
1 small apple, chopped
1 cup raisins
1/2 cup pecans, chopped

YIELD: 12
SERVING SIZE: 1
PER SERVING: Calories-183
Carbohydrate-26 g.
Protein-4 g.
Fat-8 g.
Sodium-170 mg.
EXCHANGES: 1 1/2 starch/bread, 1 1/2 fat

Roll dough into 9 x 12 inch rectangle. Spread with margarine and sprinkle with cinnamon. Spread chopped apple, raisins, and pecans over dough. Roll up like a jelly roll. Cut into 1-inch slices. Place on oiled baking sheet and let rise until nearly doubled in size. Bake at 350° for 25 to 35 minutes or until lightly browned.

135.

THE JOY OF

MUFFINS AND BREADS

Although we cannot "live by bread alone," most of us would like to try! Breads and muffins are a valuable source of carbohydrate and fiber in our diet.

Many of the breads and muffins in this section use whole wheat flour to increase the amount of fiber. They have also been modified to reduce sugar and saturated fats (polyunsaturated oil and margarine are used in place of butter and solid shortening). Here you will find a selection of delicious fruit muffins, bran muffins, quick breads, and more. They make perfect snacks, meal accompaniments, or even desserts!

Fresh Peach Muffins

1 egg
1 cup skim milk
1/4 cup margarine
1/2 cup sugar
1/4 teaspoon salt
1/4 teaspoon cinnamon
1 teaspoon lemon juice
1/4 teaspoon vanilla
1 cup all-purpose flour
3/4 cup whole wheat flour
3 teaspoons baking powder
1 cup unpeeled, chopped, fresh peaches

YIELD: 12
SERVING SIZE: 1
PER SERVING: Calories-152
Carbohydrate-25 g.
Protein-4 g.
Fat-5 g.
Sodium-163 mg.
EXCHANGES: 1 1/2 starch/bread, 1 fat

Beat egg and milk together. Add margarine, sugar, salt, cinnamon, lemon juice, and vanilla. Mix flours and baking powder and stir into milk mixture just until blended. Do not over-mix. Fold in peaches. Fill 12 paper-lined muffin cups 2/3 full. Bake at 450° about 20 minutes or until brown.

Raspberry Corn Muffins

1 cup cornmeal
1/2 cup whole wheat flour
1/2 cup all-purpose flour
1/4 teaspoon salt
2 tablespoons sugar
1 tablespoon baking powder
1 cup skim milk
1 egg
2 tablespoons oil
12 teaspoons low-sugar raspberry spread

YIELD: 12
SERVING SIZE: 1
PER SERVING: Calories-125
Carbohydrate-21 g.
Protein-3 g.
Fat-3 g.
Sodium-143 mg.
EXCHANGES: 1 1/2 starch/bread, 1 fat

Combine cornmeal, flours, salt, sugar, and baking powder in large mixing bowl. Combine milk, egg, and oil. Add to dry ingredients and mix well. Fill 12 paper-lined muffin cups 1/4 full. Place 1 teaspoon raspberry spread in the center of each. Top with rest of batter. Bake at 400° for 20 minutes or until golden brown.

Banana Muffins

1 1/4 cups all-purpose flour
1 cup whole bran cereal
3 tablespoons sugar
3 teaspoons baking powder
1 egg
1 cup fully ripe mashed bananas (2 bananas)
1/4 cup skim milk
1/4 cup oil

YIELD: 12
SERVING SIZE: 1
PER SERVING: Calories-154
Carbohydrate-22 g.
Protein-3 g.
Fat-6 g.
Sodium-118 mg.
EXCHANGES: 1 1/2 starch/bread, 1 fat

In medium bowl, stir together flour, cereal, sugar, and baking powder. In a smaller bowl, beat egg slightly. Beat in bananas, milk, and oil. Add all at once to flour mixture. Stir just until dry ingredients are moistened but lumpy. Spoon batter into 12 paper-lined muffin cups, filling them 1/2 full. Bake at 400° for about 20 minutes. Serve at once or reheat when served.

Gingerbread Pear Muffins

1 medium pear
1 teaspoon lemon juice
1 cup all-purpose flour
1 cup whole wheat flour
1/3 cup brown sugar, packed
2 teaspoons ginger
1/2 teaspoon allspice
1 teaspoon baking soda
1/3 cup lowfat buttermilk
1/2 cup molasses
1/4 cup oil
2 eggs, slightly beaten

YIELD: 18
SERVING SIZE: 1
PER SERVING: Calories-127
Carbohydrate-21 g.
Protein-3 g.
Fat-4 g.
Sodium-63 mg.
EXCHANGES: 1 1/2 starch/bread, 1 fat

Peel, core, and finely chop pear; sprinkle with lemon juice and toss. Combine flours, sugar, ginger, and allspice in a large bowl, mixing well. Dissolve soda in buttermilk; stir in molasses, oil, eggs, and pear mixture. Add to dry ingredients, mixing just until moistened. Spoon batter into paper-lined muffin cups, filling 2/3 full. Bake at 350° for 15 to 20 minutes.

Spicy Cranberry Muffins

1 1/2 cups all-purpose flour
1/2 cup whole wheat flour
2/3 cup sugar
3 teaspoons baking powder
1 teaspoon salt
1/4 teaspoon cinnamon
1/4 teaspoon nutmeg
2 eggs, beaten
2/3 cup skim milk
1/3 cup oil
2 cups fresh cranberries, chopped
1 cup wheat flake cereal

Topping:
4 packets Equal brand sweetener
1/2 teaspoon cinnamon

YIELD: 18
SERVING SIZE: 1
PER SERVING: Calories-143
Carbohydrate-22 g.
Protein-3 g.
Fat-5 g.
Sodium-197 mg.
EXCHANGES: 1 1/2 starch/bread, 1 fat

Combine flours, sugar, baking powder, salt, cinnamon, and nutmeg. Mix together eggs, milk, and oil and add to flour mixture. Fold in cranberries and cereal. Fill 18 paper-lined muffin cups 2/3 full. Bake at 400° for 20 minutes. Combine sweetener and cinnamon for topping; sprinkle on muffins immediately after baking.

These are a delightful Christmas muffin.

Date and Orange Muffins

1 whole seedless orange
1/2 cup unsweetened orange juice
1/2 cup unsweetened chopped dates
1 egg
1/2 cup margarine
1/2 cup whole wheat flour
1 cup all-purpose flour
1 teaspoon baking soda
1 teaspoon baking powder
1/2 cup sugar
1/2 teaspoon salt

YIELD: 18
SERVING SIZE: 1
PER SERVING: Calories-126
Carbohydrate-19 g.
Protein-2 g.
Fat-6 g.
Sodium-189 mg.
EXCHANGES: 1 starch/bread, 1 fat

Without peeling orange, cut into pieces and drop into blender. Blend until rind is finely ground. Add juice, dates, egg, and margarine and whirl again. In a bowl, combine flours, soda, baking powder, sugar, and salt. Pour orange mixture over dry ingredients and stir lightly. Fill 18 paper-lined muffin cups 2/3 full. Bake at 400° for 15 minutes.

Whole Wheat Pineapple Muffins

1 8-ounce can unsweetened crushed pineapple
1 cup whole wheat flour
1 cup all-purpose flour
2 1/4 teaspoons baking powder
1/4 teaspoon baking soda
1/2 teaspoon salt
1/4 cup sugar
1 teaspoon cinnamon
1/4 cup unsweetened orange juice
1/4 cup oil
1 egg

YIELD: 12
SERVING SIZE: 1
PER SERVING: Calories-150
Carbohydrate-23 g.
Protein-3 g.
Fat-5 g.
Sodium-175 mg.
EXCHANGES: 1 1/2 starch/bread, 1 fat

Drain pineapple and reserve liquid. Combine dry ingredients in large bowl. Add orange juice to drained pineapple juice to make 3/4 cup; combine with oil and egg. Make a well in center of dry ingredients and add liquid all at once. Stir until dry ingredients are moistened, and then stir in crushed pineapple; do not over-mix. Fill 12 paper-lined muffin cups 2/3 full. Bake at 400° for 15 minutes. Serve hot.

Carrot Pineapple Muffins

1 1/2 cups all-purpose flour
1 teaspoon baking soda
1 teaspoon baking powder
1 teaspoon cinnamon
1/2 teaspoon salt
2 eggs
1/3 cup margarine, melted
1/4 cup honey
1 teaspoon vanilla
1 cup grated carrots
1 8-ounce can unsweetened crushed pineapple

YIELD: 12
SERVING SIZE: 1
PER SERVING: Calories-190
Carbohydrate-31 g.
Protein-3 g.
Fat-6 g.
Sodium-275 mg.
EXCHANGES: 2 starch/bread, 1 fat

In mixing bowl, combine flour, soda, baking powder, cinnamon, and salt. Beat together eggs, melted margarine, honey, and vanilla. Add to dry ingredients, stirring until mixture is blended. Stir in grated carrots and undrained crushed pineapple. Fill prepared muffin cups 2/3 full. Bake at 400° for 20 minutes.

Oat Bran Muffins

2 1/4 cups Mother's Oat Bran cereal, uncooked
1/4 cup packed brown sugar
1 tablespoon baking powder
1/2 teaspoon salt
3/4 cup skim milk
2 eggs, beaten
1/4 cup honey
2 tablespoons oil
1/2 cup raisins

YIELD: 12
SERVING SIZE: 1
PER SERVING: Calories–158
Carbohydrate–25 g.
Protein–2 g.
Fat–4 g.
Sodium–198 mg.
EXCHANGES: 1 1/2 starch/bread, 1 fat

Combine dry ingredients. Add milk, eggs, honey, and oil; mix just until moistened. Stir in raisins. Fill 12 paper-lined muffin cups 3/4 full; bake at 425° for 15 minutes until golden brown.

A high fiber muffin.

Refrigerator All Bran Muffins

2 cups Nabisco 100% Bran cereal
2 cups boiling water
1 cup oil
3 whole eggs, well beaten
1 quart lowfat buttermilk
5 cups all-purpose flour
2 cups sugar
2 teaspoons baking soda
1 teaspoon baking powder
2 teaspoons salt
2 teaspoons nutmeg
4 teaspoons cinnamon
4 cups Kellogg's All-Bran cereal

YIELD: 56
SERVING SIZE: 1
PER SERVING: Calories-137
Carbohydrate-23 g.
Protein-3 g.
Fat-5 g.
Sodium-219 mg.
EXCHANGES: 1 1/2 starch/bread, 1 fat

In small bowl, pour boiling water over Nabisco bran cereal and set aside. Combine oil, eggs, and buttermilk in large bowl. Combine flour, sugar, soda, baking powder, salt, nutmeg, and cinnamon. Add to oil mixture. Stir in soaked bran cereal and Kellogg's All-Bran cereal. Stir just enough to moisten and evenly distribute liquid. Batter can be stored in refrigerator in an airtight container for up to 6 weeks. After storing, do not stir batter; spoon out as needed. Bake in paper-lined muffin cups for 15 to 20 minutes at 400°.

Bran Muffins

1 cup whole wheat flour
1/2 cup old fashioned rolled oats
1 cup unprocessed bran
1 tablespoon baking powder
3 tablespoons dark molasses
1 cup mashed bananas (2 bananas)
1 cup skim milk
1 egg
2/3 cup raisins

YIELD: 16
SERVING SIZE: 1
PER SERVING: Calories-86
Carbohydrate-19 g.
Protein-3 g.
Fat-1 g.
Sodium-76 mg.
EXCHANGES: 1 starch/bread

Combine all dry ingredients. Add rest of ingredients except raisins and mix well. Fold in raisins. Pour or spoon batter into 16 paper-lined muffin cups, filling 2/3 full. Bake at 400° for 15 to 20 minutes.

Peanut Butter Apple Muffins

2 cups all-purpose flour
4 teaspoons baking powder
3/4 teaspoon salt
1 teaspoon cinnamon
3/4 teaspoon nutmeg
3 tablespoons oil
1/4 cup peanut butter
1/2 cup sugar
1 egg
1 cup skim milk
1 cup chopped unpeeled apple

Topping:
3 packets Equal brand sweetener
1/4 teaspoon cinnamon

YIELD: 16
SERVING SIZE: 1
PER SERVING: Calories-149
Carbohydrate-22 g.
Protein-4 g.
Fat-5 g.
Sodium-218 mg.
EXCHANGES: 1 1/2 starch/bread, 1 fat

Combine flour, baking powder, salt, cinnamon, and nutmeg. In a separate bowl, blend oil and peanut butter together. Gradually add sugar. Beat until fluffy. Add egg and beat well. Stir in milk and apple. Add flour mixture all at once. Stir enough to just moisten ingredients. Fill paper-lined muffin cups 2/3 full. Bake at 400° for 20 minutes. For topping, blend 3 packets of sweetener and 1/4 teaspoon cinnamon. Sprinkle on tops of muffins immediately after baking.

Pumpkin Muffins

1 cup raisins
1/2 cup unsweetened orange juice
2 eggs
1 cup canned pumpkin
1/2 cup sugar
1/2 teaspoon ground cloves
1 teaspoon cinnamon
1/2 teaspoon salt
1/3 cup oil
1 cup all-purpose flour
3/4 cup whole wheat flour
1 1/2 teaspoons baking powder
1/2 teaspoon baking soda

YIELD: 18
SERVING SIZE: 1
PER SERVING: Calories-142
Carbohydrate-23 g.
Protein-3 g.
Fat-5 g.
Sodium-110 mg.
EXCHANGES: 1 1/2 starch/bread, 1 fat

Soak raisins in orange juice for 5 minutes. Do not drain. In large mixing bowl, beat eggs; stir in pumpkin, sugar, cloves, cinnamon, and salt. Add oil, mixing well. Stir together flours, baking powder, and soda. Add to pumpkin mixture with the raisin-orange juice mixture and stir to mix. Fill paper-lined muffin cups 2/3 full. Bake at 400° for about 25 minutes.

Sweet Potato Muffins

1 3/4 cups all-purpose flour
1/2 teaspoon salt
3 teaspoons baking powder
2 eggs, beaten
2/3 cup skim milk
1 cup mashed cooked sweet potato
3 tablespoons honey
3 tablespoons margarine, melted
1/3 cup sunflower seeds
1/3 cup raisins

YIELD: 12
SERVING SIZE: 1
PER SERVING: Calories-186
Carbohydrate-27 g.
Protein-5 g.
Fat-7 g.
Sodium-259 mg.
EXCHANGES: 2 starch/bread, 1 fat

In mixing bowl, combine flour, salt, and baking powder. Combine eggs, milk, mashed potatoes, honey, and melted margarine. Add to dry ingredients, stirring until blended. Stir in sunflower seeds and raisins. Fill prepared muffin cups 2/3 full. Bake at 400° for 20 to 25 minutes.

Cheddar Muffins

1 cup all-purpose flour
1 cup whole wheat flour
1 tablespoon baking powder
1/2 teaspoon baking soda
1/2 cup grated cheddar cheese
1/2 cup grated part skim mozzarella cheese
1 egg
1/4 cup honey
1/4 cup margarine, melted
1 cup skim buttermilk

YIELD: 12
SERVING SIZE: 1
PER SERVING: Calories-179
Carbohydrate-21 g.
Protein-7 g.
Fat-8 g.
Sodium-276 mg.
EXCHANGES: 1 1/2 starch/bread, 1 1/2 fat

In mixing bowl, combine flours, baking powder, and soda. Stir in cheeses. Beat together egg, honey, melted margarine, and buttermilk. Add to dry ingredients, stirring until mixture is blended. Fill prepared muffin cups 2/3 full. Bake at 425° for 20 minutes.

Pineapple Honey Loaf

1/4 cup margarine, softened
1/3 cup brown sugar
1 egg
2 cups all-purpose flour
1 teaspoon baking soda
1/2 teaspoon salt
1/4 cup unsweetened orange juice concentrate
1 8-ounce can unsweetened crushed pineapple, drained, reserving juice
1 tablespoon honey

YIELD: 1 loaf (16 slices)
SERVING SIZE: 1 slice
PER SERVING: Calories-113
Carbohydrate-19 g.
Protein-2 g.
Fat-3 g.
Sodium-162 mg.
EXCHANGES: 1 starch/bread, 1/2 fat

Cream together margarine and brown sugar. Add egg and beat well. Combine flour, soda, and salt. Combine orange juice concentrate, reserved pineapple juice, and honey. Alternately add dry ingredients and juice mixture to creamed mixture, beginning and ending with dry ingredients. Fold in crushed pineapple. Spread in oiled 9 x 5 x 3 inch loaf pan. Bake at 350° for 55 to 60 minutes.

Strawberry Holiday Bread

3/4 cup margarine, softened
1 cup sugar
4 eggs
1 teaspoon vanilla
3 cups all-purpose flour
1 teaspoon baking powder
1 teaspoon salt
1/2 teaspoon baking soda
2/3 cup low-sugar strawberry spread
1/3 cup plain lowfat yogurt

YIELD: 2 loaves (14 slices each)
SERVING SIZE: 1 slice
PER SERVING: Calories-138
Carbohydrate-19 g.
Protein-2 g.
Fat-6 g.
Sodium-181 mg.
EXCHANGES: 1 starch/bread, 1 fat

Cream together margarine and sugar. Add eggs one at a time, beating after each addition. Add vanilla. Combine flour, baking powder, salt, and soda. Combine strawberry spread and yogurt. Alternately add dry ingredients and strawberry mixture to creamed mixture beginning and ending with dry ingredients. Spread into 2 oiled 9 x 5 x 3 inch loaf pans. Bake at 325° for 50 to 60 minutes.

A perfect addition to holiday meals.

Applesauce Walnut Bread

3 cups whole wheat flour
3 cups all-purpose flour
1 cup whole bran cereal
3/4 cup brown sugar
1/2 teaspoon salt
1 teaspoon baking soda
1 teaspoon cinnamon
2 packages dry yeast
1/2 cup skim milk
1/2 cup water
1/3 cup margarine, melted
1 cup unsweetened applesauce, room temperature
2 eggs, room temperature
1 cup chopped walnuts

YIELD: 2 loaves (16 slices each)
SERVING SIZE: 1 slice
PER SERVING: Calories-163
Carbohydrate-26 g.
Protein-4 g.
Fat-5 g.
Sodium-90 mg.
EXCHANGES: 1 1/2 starch/bread, 1 fat

Combine flours. Mix 1 cup flour with cereal, brown sugar, salt, baking soda, cinnamon, and undissolved yeast. Heat milk, water, and margarine to 120° to 130°. Add to dry ingredients and beat 2 minutes on medium speed. Add applesauce, eggs, and 1 cup flour. Beat at high speed for 2 minutes. Stir in walnuts and remaining flour to make soft dough. Cover; let rise in warm, draft-free place until doubled, about one hour. Stir batter down, divide equally between two well-oiled 1 1/2 quart casseroles. Cover; let rise until doubled again (about one hour). Bake at 350° for 35 minutes or until done. Remove from casseroles and cool on wire rack.

Applesauce Bread (or Muffins)

1 cup raisins
1/2 cup unsweetened orange juice
1/4 cup margarine
1 cup plain lowfat yogurt
1 egg
1/2 cup sugar
1 teaspoon vanilla
1 cup unsweetened applesauce
2 cups whole wheat flour
1 1/2 teaspoons baking powder
1/2 teaspoon nutmeg
1/2 teaspoon cinnamon
1/4 teaspoon ground cloves

YIELD: 1 loaf (18 slices) or 18 muffins
SERVING SIZE: 1 slice or 1 muffin
PER SERVING: Calories–106
Carbohydrate–19 g.
Protein–3 g.
Fat–3 g.
Sodium–72 mg.
EXCHANGES: 1 starch/bread, 1/2 fat

Place raisins in a bowl and cover with orange juice until they soften. Melt margarine and combine with yogurt. Beat in egg. Add sugar and vanilla. Stir in raisin-orange juice mixture and applesauce. Mix together flour, baking powder, and spices. Gradually add flour mixture to liquid ingredients and beat until smooth.

For bread: Pour batter into an oiled and floured 9 x 5 x 3 inch loaf pan and bake at 350° for 60 minutes or until toothpick inserted in center comes out clean. Cool before slicing.

For muffins: Pour batter into paper-lined muffin cups. Bake for 25 to 30 minutes or until a toothpick inserted in center comes out clean.

Blueberry Banana Bread

2 cups whole wheat flour
1 cup all-purpose flour
1 1/3 cups sugar
4 teaspoons baking powder
1/2 teaspoon salt
1 1/2 cups quick-cooking rolled oats
2/3 cup oil
4 eggs, slightly beaten
2 cups mashed bananas (4 bananas)
2 cups fresh or frozen blueberries

YIELD: 2 loaves (16 slices each)
SERVING SIZE: 1 slice
PER SERVING: Calories-157
Carbohydrate-24 g.
Protein-3 g.
Fat-5 g.
Sodium-39 mg.
EXCHANGES: 1 1/2 starch/bread, 1 fat

Mix together flours, sugar, baking powder, and salt. Stir in oats. Add oil, eggs, bananas, and blueberries (if using frozen blueberries, do not thaw). Stir just until mixed. Pour batter into two oiled 9 x 5 x 3 inch loaf pans and bake at 350° for approximately 60 minutes or until toothpick inserted in the center comes out clean. Cool 10 minutes, remove from pans. Wrap and refrigerate several hours before slicing.

Banana Coconut Bread

1 cup all-purpose flour
1/2 cup whole wheat flour
2 teaspoons baking powder
1/2 teaspoon baking soda
1/2 teaspoon salt
1/2 teaspoon cinnamon
1/2 cup unsweetened shredded coconut
2 medium bananas, mashed
1/3 cup plain lowfat yogurt
1/4 cup margarine, melted
2 tablespoons honey
1/3 cup raisins

YIELD: 1 loaf (14 slices)
SERVING SIZE: 1 slice
PER SERVING: Calories–123
Carbohydrate–19 g.
Protein–2 g.
Fat–5 g.
Sodium–216 mg.
EXCHANGES: 1 starch/bread, 1 fat

In mixing bowl, combine flours, whole wheat flour, baking powder, soda, salt, and cinnamon. Stir in coconut. Combine bananas, yogurt, margarine, and honey. Add to dry ingredients, stirring until blended. Stir in raisins. Spread in oiled 9 x 5 x 3 inch loaf pan. Bake at 350° for 50 to 55 minutes. Cool 10 minutes in pan, then turn out onto cooling rack. This bread is best when wrapped and stored in refrigerator.

Cinnamon Carrot Bread

1/4 cup margarine
1/4 cup honey
1 egg
1 banana, mashed
1 teaspoon vanilla
1/3 cup plain lowfat yogurt
1 cup all-purpose flour
1 cup whole wheat flour
1 teaspoon baking soda
1 teaspoon baking powder
1/2 teaspoon cinnamon
1/4 teaspoon salt
1 cup grated carrots

YIELD: 1 loaf (16 slices)
SERVING SIZE: 1 slice
PER SERVING: Calories-110
Carbohydrate-18 g.
Protein-3 g.
Fat-4 g.
Sodium-160 mg.
EXCHANGES: 1 starch/bread, 1 fat

Cream together margarine and honey. Beat in egg, banana, vanilla, and yogurt. Combine flours, soda, baking powder, cinnamon, and salt. Add to creamed mixture, blending well. Stir in grated carrots. Batter will be slightly stiff. Pour into oiled 9 x 5 x 3 inch loaf pan. Bake at 350° for 50 to 60 minutes.

Honey Bran Nut Bread

1 cup whole bran cereal
1 1/3 cups skim milk
2 eggs, beaten
1/3 cup margarine, melted
1/4 cup honey
2 cups whole wheat flour
1 teaspoon baking powder
1/2 teaspoon baking soda
1/2 teaspoon salt
1/3 cup sunflower seeds

YIELD: 1 loaf (16 slices)
SERVING SIZE: 1 slice
PER SERVING: Calories–156
Carbohydrate–21 g.
Protein–5 g.
Fat–7 g.
Sodium–250 mg.
EXCHANGES: 1 1/2 starch/bread, 1 fat

In large mixing bowl, stir together cereal and milk. Let stand until cereal is softened, about 2 minutes. Add eggs, melted margarine, and honey. Beat well. Combine flour, baking powder, soda, and salt. Add to cereal mixture, stirring until blended. Add sunflower seeds. Pour into oiled 9 x 5 x 3 inch loaf pan. Bake at 350° for 60 to 65 minutes.

Oatmeal Quick Bread

1 1/2 cups whole wheat flour
1 cup all-purpose flour
1/2 cup quick-cooking rolled oats
1/3 cup packed brown sugar
1 tablespoon grated orange rind
2 teaspoons baking powder
1/2 teaspoon baking soda
1 3/4 cups soured milk*
1 egg white
2 tablespoons sunflower seeds
2 tablespoons wheat germ

**Add 2 tablespoons lemon juice or vinegar to milk to sour.*

YIELD: 1 loaf (12 slices)
SERVING SIZE: 1 slice
PER SERVING: Calories-147
Carbohydrate-29 g.
Protein-6 g.
Fat-1 g.
Sodium-112 mg.
EXCHANGES: 2 starch/bread

In large bowl, combine flours, oats, brown sugar, orange rind, baking powder, and baking soda and blend well. Add soured milk and egg white; stir until ingredients are just moistened. Stir in sunflower seeds. Sprinkle wheat germ into oiled 1 1/2 quart casserole. Pour batter into casserole. Bake at 350° for 50 to 60 minutes until bread tests done. If necessary, cover loaf with foil during last 15 minutes to prevent over-browning. Cool in casserole for 10 minutes. Serve warm or cool.

Graham Date Bread

1 1/4 cups all-purpose flour
1 2/3 cups graham cracker crumbs
1 tablespoon baking soda
1 tablespoon cinnamon
1/2 cup margarine, softened
1/4 teaspoon salt
1/3 cup sugar
2 eggs
1 cup unsweetened orange juice
2 teaspoons grated orange rind
1 cup chopped unsweetened dates
1 cup chopped walnuts

YIELD: 1 loaf (16 slices)
SERVING SIZE: 1 slice
PER SERVING: Calories-195
Carbohydrate-29 g.
Protein-4 g.
Fat-7 g.
Sodium-321 mg.
EXCHANGES: 2 starch/bread, 1 fat

Combine all ingredients except dates and walnuts in large bowl. Blend until dry ingredients are moistened. Beat at medium speed for 3 minutes. Stir in dates and nuts. Place in an oiled and floured 9 x 5 x 3 inch loaf pan. Bake at 350° for 65 minutes or until toothpick inserted in center comes out clean. Cool 10 minutes before removing from pan. Cool completely before serving.

Pumpkin Bread

1/2 cup oil
2 cups sugar
4 eggs
1 16-ounce can pumpkin
1 cup water
2 cups whole wheat flour
1 1/2 cups all-purpose flour
2 teaspoons baking soda
1 teaspoon salt
1/2 teaspoon baking powder
1 teaspoon cinnamon
1 teaspoon ground cloves
1/2 cup chopped walnuts
1 cup raisins

YIELD: 3 loaves (15 slices each)
SERVING SIZE: 1 slice
PER SERVING: Calories-120
Carbohydrate-20 g.
Protein-2 g.
Fat-4 g.
Sodium-94 mg.
EXCHANGES: 1 starch/bread, 1 fat

Cream oil and sugar until fluffy. Stir in eggs, pumpkin, and water. Blend in flours, soda, salt, baking powder, and spices. Stir in nuts and raisins. Pour into three oiled 9 x 5 x 3 inch pans. Bake at 350° for 60 to 70 minutes. Cool before slicing.

Kids will love this for Halloween.

Sunflower Zucchini Bread

3 eggs
1 cup oil
1 1/2 cups sugar
2 cups zucchini, peeled and grated
1 tablespoon vanilla
1 tablespoon molasses
1 1/2 cups all-purpose flour
1 1/2 cups whole wheat flour
1 teaspoon salt
1/4 teaspoon baking soda
4 teaspoons cinnamon
1/2 cup sunflower seeds, chopped

YIELD: 2 loaves (16 slices each)
SERVING SIZE: 1 slice
PER SERVING: Calories-162
Carbohydrate-19 g.
Protein-3 g.
Fat-9 g.
Sodium-80 mg.
EXCHANGES: 1 starch/bread, 2 fat

Beat eggs until lemon-colored. Gradually pour in oil, beating well. Add sugar, zucchini, vanilla, and molasses. Beat well. Combine flours, salt, soda, and cinnamon. Add dry ingredients to egg mixture, combining only until well blended. Stir in chopped sunflower seeds. Pour into two 9 x 5 x 3 inch loaf pans. Bake at 350° for about 50 minutes. Cool for 10 minutes in pans, then remove.

THE JOY OF COOKIES AND BARS

The craving for cookies that lurks within all of us is satisfied with these recipes. Many use fresh and dried fruits for sweetness rather than sugar. Cereals, oats, nuts, and whole wheat flour are other ingredients that increase the fiber content of these cookies and bars.

Oatmeal Cookies

1/3 cup margarine
1/3 cup lightly packed brown sugar
1/4 cup warm water
1/2 teaspoon vanilla
1 cup all-purpose flour
1 cup quick-cooking rolled oats
1 1/4 teaspoons cinnamon
1/2 teaspoon baking powder

YIELD: 24
SERVING SIZE: 2
PER SERVING: Calories-132
Carbohydrate-18 g.
Protein-2 g.
Fat-6 g.
Sodium-98 mg.
EXCHANGES: 1 starch/bread, 1 fat

Cream together margarine and sugar until light and fluffy. Beat in water and vanilla. Combine flour, oats, cinnamon, and baking powder. Stir into creamed mixture. Roll out 1/8-inch thick on a lightly floured surface. Cut into 24 circles 2 1/2 inches in diameter and place on a lightly oiled baking sheet. Bake at 350° for 10 to 12 minutes, until golden brown around the edges. Cool and store in a covered container.

168.

Oatmeal Chocolate Chip Cookies

1/3 cup margarine
1/4 cup granulated brown sugar substitute
1/4 cup brown sugar
1 egg
3 teaspoons vanilla
3/4 cup all-purpose flour
1/2 teaspoon baking soda
1/4 teaspoon salt
3/4 cup quick-cooking rolled oats
1/3 cup chocolate chips

YIELD: 34
SERVING SIZE: 2
PER SERVING: Calories-127
Carbohydrate-16 g.
Protein-2 g.
Fat-6 g.
Sodium-103 mg.
EXCHANGES: 1 starch/bread, 1 fat

Cream together margarine, brown sugar substitute, and brown sugar until light and fluffy. Beat in egg and vanilla. Combine flour, baking soda, and salt. Stir into creamed mixture. Fold in rolled oats and chocolate chips. Using 2 teaspoons for each cookie, drop onto ungreased baking sheet. Flatten with fork. Bake at 375° for 10 minutes until cookies begin to brown around the edges. Store in a covered container.

Oatmeal Raisin Cookies

1/2 cup water
1 cup raisins
1/2 cup oil
3/4 cup brown sugar
1/4 cup white sugar
2 eggs
1 cup whole wheat flour
1 cup all-purpose flour
1 teaspoon baking soda
1 teaspoon cinnamon
1/2 teaspoon nutmeg
1/3 teaspoon allspice
1/2 teaspoon salt
2 cups quick-cooking rolled oats

YIELD: 48
SERVING SIZE: 2
PER SERVING: Calories-160
Carbohydrate-26 g.
Protein-2 g.
Fat-6 g.
Sodium-84 mg.
EXCHANGES: 2 starch/bread, 1 fat

Combine water and raisins in a saucepan and heat until the water begins to boil; turn off heat and cool. Combine oil, sugar, and eggs and beat well. Add raisins and all liquid to mixture. Add dry ingredients. Beat well and stir in oats. Drop by rounded teaspoonfuls onto oiled baking sheet. Bake at 350° for 10 to 12 minutes or until delicately brown.

Raisin Drop Cookies

1 tablespoon liquid artificial sweetener
2/3 cup unsweetened orange juice
1/4 cup oil
1 cup raisins
1 teaspoon cinnamon
1/4 teaspoon nutmeg
1 teaspoon grated orange peel
1/4 teaspoon salt
1 egg
1/2 cup whole wheat flour
1/2 cup all-purpose flour
1 teaspoon baking powder

YIELD: 24
SERVING SIZE: 2
PER SERVING: Calories-126
Carbohydrate-19 g.
Protein-2 g.
Fat-5 g.
Sodium-56 mg.
EXCHANGES: 1 starch/bread, 1 fat

In medium saucepan, combine the sweetener, orange juice, oil, raisins, cinnamon, nutmeg, and orange peel. Boil for 3 minutes. Let mixture cool. Add salt. Beat in egg. Combine flours and baking powder; add to mixture, mixing well. Drop by rounded teaspoonfuls onto baking sheet. Bake at 350° until light brown.

Spicy Ginger Cookies

1/3 cup margarine
1/2 cup honey
1 egg
1 tablespoon molasses
1 teaspoon vinegar
1 3/4 cups all-purpose flour
3/4 teaspoon baking soda
1 1/2 teaspoons ginger
1/4 teaspoon ground gloves

YIELD: 30
SERVING SIZE: 2
PER SERVING: Calories-124
Carbohydrate-20 g.
Protein-2 g.
Fat-4 g.
Sodium- 94 mg.
EXCHANGES: 1 starch/bread, 1 fat

Cream together margarine and honey. Beat in egg, molasses, and vinegar. Combine flour, soda, and spices; add to creamed mixture and blend. Drop by teaspoonfuls onto oiled baking sheets. Bake at 350° for 10 to 12 minutes.

Delicate Orange Tea Cookies

1/2 cup sugar
1/3 cup margarine
1/3 cup plain lowfat yogurt
1 egg
2 cups all-purpose flour
1/2 teaspoon baking soda
1/2 teaspoon baking powder
1/4 teaspoon salt
2 tablespoons unsweetened orange juice concentrate
3 tablespoons water
1 tablespoon grated orange rind

YIELD: 42
SERVING SIZE: 2
PER SERVING: Calories-92
Carbohydrate-14 g.
Protein-2 g.
Fat-4 g.
Sodium-98 mg.
EXCHANGES: 1 starch/bread, 1 fat

Cream sugar and margarine. Add yogurt and egg. Combine flour, soda, baking powder, and salt. Set aside. Combine orange juice concentrate, water, and orange rind. Gradually add dry ingredients to creamed mixture alternately with the orange juice mixture. Mix well. Drop by teaspoonfuls onto slightly oiled baking sheet. Bake at 350° for 8 to 10 minutes. Quickly remove from baking sheet. When cool, frost each cookie with 1/2 teaspoon Orange Frosting.

Orange Frosting: In small bowl, combine 2 tablespoons soft margarine, 3/4 cup powdered sugar, 1 teaspoon grated orange rind, and 1 1/2 teaspoons orange juice. This recipe makes 7 tablespoons of frosting, enough to frost each cookie with 1/2 teaspoon.

One of our favorites, these cookies are perfect for a party or reception.

Apple Cheese Cookies

3/4 cup all-purpose flour
1/4 cup brown sugar
3/4 teaspoon cinnamon
1/2 teaspoon baking powder
1/2 teaspoon salt
2 tablespoons wheat germ
1/2 cup margarine, softened
1 egg
1 teaspoon vanilla
1 1/2 cups quick-cooking rolled oats
1/2 cup shredded cheddar cheese
1/2 cup shredded part skim mozzarella cheese
1/2 cup raisins
3/4 cup chopped baking apple

YIELD: 36
SERVING SIZE: 2
PER SERVING: Calories-150
Carbohydrate-16 g.
Protein-2 g.
Fat-10 g.
Sodium-180 mg.
EXCHANGES: 1 starch/bread, 2 fat

In large bowl, stir together flour, brown sugar, cinnamon, baking powder, salt, and wheat germ. Add margarine, egg, and vanilla, mixing well. Stir in oats, cheeses, raisins, and chopped apple. Drop onto baking sheet, allowing only 2 teaspoons of dough for each cookie. Bake at 375° for 10 to 12 minutes. Remove from baking sheet. To store, place in airtight container. May be frozen.

Cheesy cookies that are sure to please any age.

Ginger Spice Cookies

1/4 cup oil
2 tablespoons margarine
1 tablespoon skim milk
1 egg
1/2 teaspoon vanilla
1/2 teaspoon ginger
1/4 teaspoon ground cloves
1/2 teaspoon cinnamon
1 1/2 cups all-purpose flour
1/2 teaspoon salt

Coating:
12 packets Equal brand sweetener
1/2 teaspoon cinnamon

YIELD: 36
SERVING SIZE: 3
PER SERVING: Calories-112
Carbohydrate-13 g.
Protein-2 g.
Fat-7 g.
Sodium-146 mg.
EXCHANGES: 1 starch/bread, 1 fat

Beat together oil and margarine. Add milk, egg, and vanilla and beat well. Combine dry ingredients, blend into liquid mixture. Roll into 3/4-inch balls. Place cookies on ungreased baking sheet and flatten with glass to 1/8-inch thickness. Bake at 375° for 7 minutes. For coating, combine sweetener and cinnamon in plastic bag. Place warm cookies in bag and shake to coat.

Angel Macaroons

1 16-ounce one-step angel food cake mix
1/2 cup sugar-free strawberry flavored carbonated beverage
2 teaspoons vanilla or almond extract
2 cups unsweetened shredded coconut
1/2 cup chopped walnuts

YIELD: 60
SERVING SIZE: 2
PER SERVING: Calories-98
Carbohydrate-14 g.
Protein-2 g.
Fat-4 g.
Sodium-112 mg.
EXCHANGES: 1 starch/bread, 1 fat

Cover baking sheet with aluminum foil. In large mixing bowl, beat the cake mix together with the carbonated beverage and vanilla on low speed for 1/2 minute, then at medium speed for 1 minute, scraping sides of bowl. Fold in coconut and nuts. Drop by teaspoonfuls onto foil-lined baking sheet, 2 inches apart. Bake at 350° for 10 to 12 minutes. Slide foil onto cooling rack. Cool. Store in airtight containers.

Popcorn Macaroons

3 cups popped popcorn, unsalted
2 egg whites
1/4 cup sugar
1/4 teaspoon salt
1 teaspoon vanilla
1/3 cup unsweetened shredded coconut

YIELD: 24
SERVING SIZE: 2
PER SERVING: Calories-52
Carbohydrate-8 g.
Protein-1 g.
Fat-1 g.
Sodium-58 mg.
EXCHANGES: 1/2 starch/bread

Whirl popped popcorn in blender, one cup at a time, until finely ground. Pour into measuring cup; continue until there are 1 1/2 cups ground popcorn. Set aside.
In medium bowl, beat egg whites on highest speed until stiff peaks form. Add sugar gradually, beating at low speed until egg whites are glossy and stiff. Beat in salt and vanilla. Gently fold in the 1 1/2 cups ground popcorn and coconut. Drop by rounded teaspoonfuls onto oiled baking sheet. Bake at 325° for 10 to 12 minutes or until lightly browned. Quickly remove from baking sheets. Cool.

A wonderful way to use leftover popcorn!

Banana Chews

4 bananas
1/2 cup quick-cooking rolled oats
1 cup chopped dried apple
1 1/2 cups chopped peanuts
1 teaspoon vanilla
1 teaspoon cinnamon

YIELD: 24
SERVING SIZE: 1
PER SERVING: Calories-82
Carbohydrate-9 g.
Protein-3 g.
Fat-5 g.
Sodium-1 mg.
EXCHANGES: 1/2 fruit, 1 fat

Mash bananas and add other ingredients. Mix well. Drop by rounded teaspoonfuls onto ungreased baking sheet. Bake at 350° for 20 to 25 minutes.

Spicy Walnut Chews

1 cup whole wheat flour
1 teaspoon baking powder
1/2 teaspoon baking soda
1/2 teaspoon salt
1 teaspoon pumpkin pie spice
1/2 cup margarine, softened
1/3 cup honey
2 eggs
1/3 cup unsweetened applesauce
1/4 cup molasses
1 3/4 cups quick-cooking rolled oats
1/2 cup chopped walnuts

YIELD: 36
SERVING SIZE: 2
PER SERVING: Calories-134
Carbohydrate-17 g.
Protein-2 g.
Fat-8 g.
Sodium-68 mg.
EXCHANGES: 1 starch/bread, 1 1/2 fat

Combine flour, baking powder, soda, salt, and spice. In large bowl, cream together margarine and honey. Add eggs one at a time. Blend in applesauce, then molasses. Stir in flour mixture and oats, blending well. Fold in walnuts. Drop by teaspoonfuls onto oiled baking sheets. Bake at 350° for 10 to 12 minutes or until lightly browned. Let stand on cookie sheets about 5 minutes, then place on cooling racks.

An old fashioned oatmeal cookie!

Oatmeal Honey Gems

1/3 cup honey
1 tablespoon oil
2 eggs
1 teaspoon almond extract
1 tablespoon grated orange peel
1/2 teaspoon salt
1 1/2 cups quick-cooking rolled oats
1 cup unsweetened shredded coconut

YIELD: 24
SERVING SIZE: 2
PER SERVING: Calories-114
Carbohydrate-15 g.
Protein-3 g.
Fat-5 g.
Sodium-101 mg.
EXCHANGES: 1 starch/bread, 1 fat

Mix honey, oil, and eggs with a wire wisk in deep bowl. Add almond extract, orange peel, salt, oats, and coconut. Stir until blended. Drop by teaspoonfuls onto oiled baking sheet. Bake at 400° for 7 minutes or until tops become light brown.

Scottish Oat Scones

1 1/2 cups all-purpose flour
1/4 cup sugar
1 tablespoon baking powder
1 teaspoon cream of tartar
1/2 teaspoon salt
1 1/4 cups quick-cooking rolled oats
1/2 cup margarine, melted
1/3 cup skim milk
1 egg
1/2 cup raisins

YIELD: 12
SERVING SIZE: 1
PER SERVING: Calories-207
Carbohydrate-28 g.
Protein-4 g.
Fat-9 g.
Sodium-275 mg.
EXCHANGES: 2 starch/bread, 2 fat

Combine flour, sugar, baking powder, cream of tartar, and salt. Add oats, margarine, milk, and egg. Mix just until dry ingredients are moistened. Stir in raisins. Shape dough to form ball; pat out on lightly floured surface to form 8-inch circle. Cut into 12 wedges (scones); bake on oiled baking sheet at 425° for 12 to 15 minutes or until light golden brown. Serve warm.

Raisin Scones

1/2 cup raisins
1/2 cup unsweetened orange juice
1 2/3 cups all-purpose flour
1/4 cup sugar
2 teaspoons baking powder
1/4 teaspoon baking soda
1/2 teaspoon salt
1/4 cup margarine
1 egg
1 teaspoon grated orange rind

YIELD: 24
SERVING SIZE: 1
PER SERVING: Calories-62
Carbohydrate-11 g.
Protein-1 g.
Fat-2 g.
Sodium-118 mg.
EXCHANGES: 1 starch/bread

Combine raisins and orange juice. Set aside. Combine flour, sugar, baking powder, soda, and salt. Cut margarine into dry ingredients using pastry blender until pieces are the size of small peas. Add egg, orange rind, and raisin-orange juice mixture. Mix only until all is moistened. Roll or pat into an 8 x 12 inch rectangle using up to 1/4 cup flour if needed (dough will be soft). Cut into 2-inch squares (4 across, 6 down). Place on oiled baking sheet and bake at 400° for 10 to 12 minutes.

Serve with 1/2 teaspoon low-sugar strawberry spread for extra delicious flavor.

Hawaiian Fruit Bars

1 1/4 cups unsweetened shredded coconut
1/4 cup margarine
1/3 cup honey
3 eggs
1/4 cup unsweetened orange juice concentrate
4 teaspoons vanilla
1 tablespoon grated orange rind
1 20-ounce can unsweetened crushed pineapple, undrained
2 cups plus 2 tablespoons all-purpose flour
1 teaspoon baking soda
4 teaspoons baking powder
1/2 teaspoon salt
1/3 cup finely chopped walnuts

YIELD: 60
SERVING SIZE: 3
PER SERVING: Calories-84
Carbohydrate-6 g.
Protein-2 g.
Fat-6 g.
Sodium-153 mg.
EXCHANGES: 1/2 fruit, 1 fat

Toast coconut in shallow baking pan at 300° for 8 to 9 minutes, until lightly brown; stirring often. Beat together margarine, honey, eggs, and orange juice concentrate. Add vanilla, orange rind, and crushed pineapple with juice. Sift together flour, soda, baking powder, and salt. Gradually blend into creamed mixture. Fold in toasted coconut and nuts. Pour into oiled 10 x 15 inch baking pan. Bake at 325° for 40 to 45 minutes. Cut into 60 bars (10 down and 6 across).

Cottage Cheese Strawberry Squares

1/3 cup margarine, softened
1/2 cup lowfat cottage cheese, small curd
1 cup all-purpose flour
2/3 cup low-sugar strawberry spread

YIELD: 32
SERVING SIZE: 2
PER SERVING: Calories-84
Carbohydrate-10 g.
Protein-2 g.
Fat-4 g.
Sodium-86 mg.
EXCHANGES: 1/2 starch/bread, 1 fat

In small mixing bowl, cream together margarine and cottage cheese. Stir in flour, mixing well. Wrap dough in waxed paper and chill until firm. Divide dough in half; roll each half to a 12 x 12 inch square. Cut each half into 16 squares. Place 1 teaspoon of strawberry spread in center of each square. Pull corners of each square over strawberry spread, sealing edges firmly. Bake at 350° for 15 to 18 minutes until edges are brown.

So quick and so good—these are great any time of the day.

Tasty Granola Bars

3/4 cup Grape-Nuts cereal
1 1/4 cups quick-cooking rolled oats
1 cup raisins
1/2 cup peanut butter
4 teaspoons honey
1/2 cup unsweetened grape juice

YIELD: 12
SERVING SIZE: 1
PER SERVING: Calories-180
Carbohydrate-30 g.
Protein-5 g.
Fat-5 g.
Sodium-66 mg.
EXCHANGES: 2 starch/bread, 1 fat

Mix together cereal, oats, raisins, peanut butter, and honey. Stir in grape juice. (If too dry, add 1 to 2 more teaspoons juice.) Divide mixture into 12 portions. Cut 12 squares of foil and put 1 portion of cookie mixture on each square. Flatten mixture into bar shape. Wrap. Freeze. Eat frozen.

Variation: Substitute 1/2 cup unsweetened orange juice and 1/2 banana, mashed, for grape juice. Make as directed.

(Your Own) Granola Bars

3 1/2 cups quick-cooking rolled oats
1 cup raisins (optional)
1/2 cup chopped nuts
2/3 cup margarine, melted
1/4 cup brown sugar, firmly packed
1/4 cup honey
1 egg, beaten
1/2 teaspoon vanilla
1/2 teaspoon salt

YIELD: 30
SERVING SIZE: 1
PER SERVING: Calories-115
Carbohydrate-15 g.
Protein-2 g.
Fat-6 g.
Sodium-90 mg.
EXCHANGES: 1 starch/bread, 1 fat

Place oats on a baking sheet and bake at 350° for 15 to 20 minutes or until light golden brown. Combine all ingredients and mix well. Place firmly into a 15 x 10 inch jelly roll pan sprayed with low calorie cooking spray. Bake at 350° for 20 minutes. Cool. Store in tightly covered container in cool, dry place or in refrigerator.

Raisin Date Bars

1 1/2 cups unsweetened chopped dates
1 1/2 cups raisins
1 1/2 cups water
1 to 2 tablespoons grated orange rind
1 cup whole wheat flour
1 cup all-purpose flour
1 cup quick-cooking rolled oats
1 teaspoon baking soda
1/4 cup granulated brown sugar substitute
1 cup margarine

YIELD: 32
SERVING SIZE: 1
PER SERVING: Calories-132
Carbohydrate-19 g.
Protein-2 g.
Fat-6 g.
Sodium-72 mg.
EXCHANGES: 1 starch/bread, 1 fat

Cook dates and raisins in water until thick; add grated orange rind. Thoroughly mix the flours, oats, soda, brown sugar substitute, and margarine. Pat 2/3 of the dry mixture into a 9 x 13 inch pan. Spread with date mixture, then cover with remaining crumbs, pressing down slightly to help prevent crumbling when cutting. Bake at 375° for 20 to 25 minutes.

Refrigerator Oatmeal Nut Bars

1/2 cup peanut butter
2 tablespoons honey
2 eggs
2 tablespoons margarine
1 tablespoon vanilla
1/2 cup sunflower seeds
1/2 cup chopped walnuts
2 cups quick-cooking rolled oats
1/2 cup raisins

YIELD: 24
SERVING SIZE: 1
PER SERVING: Calories-115
Carbohydrate-10 g.
Protein-4 g.
Fat-7 g.
Sodium-50 mg.
EXCHANGES: 1 starch/bread, 1 fat

Mix peanut butter and honey in saucepan over medium heat. Beat in eggs one at a time. Stir constantly for 3 minutes. Remove from heat; stir in margarine and vanilla. Add nuts, oats, and raisins and mix well. Press mixture into 8-inch square pan and chill.

Chocolate Chip Snack Squares

1/3 cup margarine, softened
2 tablespoons honey
1/3 cup skim milk
1 egg
1/3 cup unsweetened orange juice concentrate
1 teaspoon vanilla
1 1/2 cups all-purpose flour
1 teaspoon baking soda
1/4 teaspoon salt
1/4 cup mini semisweet chocolate chips

YIELD: 15
SERVING SIZE: 1
PER SERVING: Calories-102
Carbohydrate-12 g.
Protein-2 g.
Fat-6 g.
Sodium-62 mg.
EXCHANGES: 1 starch/bread, 1 fat

In small mixing bowl, combine margarine, honey, milk, egg, orange juice concentrate, and vanilla. Combine flour, soda, and salt. Stir into liquid ingredients. Mix well. Fold in chocolate chips. Spread mixture in oiled and floured 8 x 8 x 2 inch pan. Bake at 350° for 20 to 25 minutes. Cut into 15 squares.

THE JOY OF PIES

Pie is always a favorite dessert, and in this section you will find pie recipes for any occasion. The secret to a successful pie is accurately measuring ingredients, properly mixing the pie filling, and baking at the correct temperature and for the correct time.

Four pie crust recipes are included to use with the pie recipes in this section. Note that oil or margarine replace solid shortening to decrease the saturated fat content of the crusts. Pie fillings in this section have been modified to reduce sugar; the sweetness comes from fruit and fruit juice concentrate.

In recipes that call for whipped topping with Equal brand sweetener, add the sweetener to the whipped topping at the end of the whipping process, since the sweetener tends to decrease the total volume of the topping. Also, use as few strokes as possible when folding beaten egg whites with other ingredients to avoid removing the air from the egg whites.

Although these pie recipes may not all be "low calorie," they are lower in calories, fat, and sugar than their unmodified counterparts.

Easy Pastry Shell

1/3 cup margarine, softened
1 tablespoon sugar
1 cup all-purpose flour

YIELD: 1 crust
SERVING SIZE: 1/8 crust
PER SERVING: Calories-136
Carbohydrate-15 g.
Protein-2 g.
Fat-7 g.
Sodium-93 mg.
EXCHANGES: 1 starch/bread, 1 fat

Combine, but do not cream, margarine and sugar. Add flour and mix until dough forms. Press evenly on bottom and sides of a 9-inch pie pan, using well-floured fingers. If a baked pie shell is needed, prick sides and bottom of crust with fork. Bake at 375° for 12 to 15 minutes until light golden brown.

Single Crust Oil Pastry

1 1/2 cups all-purpose flour
1/2 teaspoon salt
1/3 cup oil
3 tablespoons ice water

YIELD: 1 crust
SERVING SIZE: 1/8 pie
PER SERVING: Calories-173
Carbohydrate-19 g.
Protein–3 g.
Fat-9 g.
Sodium-133 mg.
EXCHANGES: 1 starch/bread, 2 fat

Stir together flour and salt. Combine oil and ice water in measuring cup. Whip with fork until thickened. Immediately pour all at once over flour mixture. Toss with fork. (Dough will be moist.) Shape into ball and roll out between two 12-inch squares of waxed paper (dampen table slightly so paper will not slip). Roll out until dough forms a circle reaching edge of paper. Remove top paper; invert 9-inch pie pan over pastry. Flip pan so pastry is on top. Fit pastry into pan and remove paper. Trim crust 1 1/2 inches beyond pan rim. Flute edges. For baked crust, generously prick bottom and sides of pastry shell with fork. Bake at 425° for 10 to 15 minutes.

Double Crust Oil Pastry

2 cups all-purpose flour
3/4 teaspoon salt
1/2 cup oil
5 tablespoons ice water

YIELD: 1 crust
SERVING SIZE: 1/8 crust
PER SERVING: Calories-245
Carbohydrate-26 g.
Protein-4 g.
Fat-14 g.
Sodium-216 mg.
EXCHANGES: 1 1/2 starch/bread, 3 fat

Stir together flour and salt. Combine oil and ice water in measuring cup. Whip with fork until thickened. Immediately pour all at once over flour mixture. Toss with fork. The dough will be moist. Shape dough into a ball and divide in half, allowing a little more dough for the bottom crust. Roll out between two 12-inch squares of waxed paper until dough forms circle, reaching edge of paper. Remove top paper and invert pie pan over pastry, then flip pan so pastry is on top. Fit into pan; remove paper. Roll out top crust. Cut holes for steam to escape. Fill with desired filling; trim crust, folding top pastry under bottom pastry. Flute edge. Bake according to directions for filling recipe.

Graham Cracker Crust

1 1/4 cups graham cracker crumbs
1/3 cup margarine, melted

YIELD: 1 crust
SERVING SIZE: 1/8 crust
PER SERVING: Calories-79
Carbohydrate-10 g.
Protein-1 g.
Fat-4 g.
Sodium-91 mg.
EXCHANGES: 1/2 starch/bread, 1 fat

Combine crumbs and margarine in 9-inch pie pan. Press firmly on sides and bottom of pan. Bake at 375° for 6 to 8 minutes, or until lightly browned.

Honey Apple Pie

2 tablespoons all-purpose flour
1/4 teaspoon nutmeg
1 teaspoon cinnamon
6 cups peeled, sliced baking apples
1/4 cup honey
1 teaspoon lemon juice
1 9-inch unbaked double crust oil pastry (see recipe page 193)

YIELD: 1 pie
SERVING SIZE: 1/8 pie
PER SERVING: Calories-306
Carbohydrate-41 g.
Protein-4 g.
Fat-14 g.
Sodium-217 mg.
EXCHANGES: 2 starch/bread, 1 fruit, 2 fat

Combine flour and spices. Sprinkle over apples, stirring to thoroughly mix. Combine honey and lemon juice. Pour over apples and mix until well blended. Turn into 9-inch unbaked pastry shell; top with second crust. Seal edges. Bake at 425° for 10 minutes, then at 375° for 40 to 45 minutes or until done.

Double Apple Pie

2 1/2 tablespoons all-purpose flour
6 cups peeled, sliced baking apples
2/3 cup unsweetened apple juice concentrate
2 teaspoons cornstarch
1 teaspoon cinnamon
1/4 teaspoon nutmeg
1 9-inch unbaked double crust oil pastry (see recipe page 193)

YIELD: 1 pie
SERVING SIZE: 1/8 pie
PER SERVING: Calories-366
Carbohydrate-46 g.
Protein-5 g.
Fat-15 g.
Sodium-217 mg.
EXCHANGES: 2 starch/bread, 1 fruit, 3 fat

Sprinkle flour over sliced apples and stir gently to combine. In saucepan, combine apple juice concentrate, cornstarch, and spices; stir until smooth. Place over medium heat and stir constantly until thickened. Pour over apples, mixing gently until all apples are coated. Pour into pastry lined pie plate and top with second crust. Seal edges. Bake at 425° for 10 minutes. Reduce heat to 375° and bake 35 to 40 minutes.

A delicious sugar-free pie!

Honey Pumpkin Pie

2 large eggs
1/4 cup honey
1 cup evaporated skim milk
1 cup cooked pumpkin
1 1/2 teaspoons pumpkin pie spice
1/4 teaspoon salt
2 teaspoons unsweetened orange juice concentrate
1 9-inch unbaked single crust oil pastry (see recipe page 192)

YIELD: 1 pie
SERVING SIZE: 1/8 pie
PER SERVING: Calories-257
Carbohydrate-33 g.
Protein-7 g.
Fat-11 g.
Sodium-271 mg.
EXCHANGES: 2 starch/bread, 2 fat

With electric mixer, beat eggs until foamy, about 1 minute. Add honey, milk, pumpkin, spice, salt, and juice concentrate. Beat until well blended. Pour pumpkin filling into unbaked pie shell. Bake at 375° for 60 to 65 minutes, or until knife inserted off center comes out clean.

Strawberry Cream Cheese Pie

1 9-inch unbaked easy or single crust oil pastry shell (see recipes page 191 and 192)
1 8-ounce package Neufchâtel cheese
2 tablespoons honey
2 eggs
1 teaspoon vanilla
1 tablespoon cornstarch
1/2 teaspoon sugar
1/3 cup cold water
1/2 cup low-sugar strawberry spread
3 cups fresh strawberries, sliced

YIELD: 1 pie
SERVING SIZE: 1/10 pie
PER SERVING: Calories-222
Carbohydrate-21 g.
Protein-5 g.
Fat-13 g.
Sodium-190 mg.
EXCHANGES: 1 starch/bread, 1/2 fruit, 2 fat

Prick bottom and sides of unbaked pastry shell. Bake at 350° for 10 to 12 minutes until pastry is golden. Beat together cheese, honey, eggs, and vanilla until well blended. Pour into partially baked crust and bake again at 350° for 18 to 20 minutes. Chill. (Cheese filling will become firm when refrigerated.) To make glaze, combine cornstarch and sugar in small saucepan; slowly blend in water. Stir mixture over low heat until thickened. Add strawberry spread, stir until well blended. Chill until almost firm. Add strawberries and spread over chilled cream cheese filling. Chill at least 2 to 3 hours.

Fresh Strawberry Pie

1 package sugar-free strawberry flavored gelatin
1 cup boiling water
3/4 cup sugar-free strawberry flavored carbonated beverage
5 cups sliced fresh strawberries
1 tablespoon sugar
1 9-inch baked easy pastry shell (see recipe page 191)

YIELD: 1 pie
SERVING SIZE: 1/10 pie
PER SERVING: Calories-136
Carbohydrate-17 g.
Protein–2 g.
Fat-6 g.
Sodium-100 mg.
EXCHANGES: 1 starch/bread, 1 fat

Combine gelatin and boiling water; stir until well blended. Add carbonated beverage, mixing well. Chill in freezer, stirring every 5 minutes, until very thick but not firm. Remove from freezer. Add 1 tablespoon sugar to strawberries. Gently fold strawberries into gelatin. Pour into baked pastry shell. Chill in refrigerator several hours until firm.

Blueberry Orange Pie

1 package sugar-free orange flavored gelatin
1 cup boiling water
2 cups plain lowfat yogurt
2 packets Equal brand sweetener
1 1/4 cups fresh or unsweetened frozen blueberries, thawed and drained
1 tablespoon powdered sugar
1 9-inch baked graham cracker crust (see recipe page 194)
1 envelope reduced calorie whipped topping mix

YIELD: 1 pie
SERVING SIZE: 1/8 pie
PER SERVING: Calories-165
Carbohydrate-19 g.
Protein-4 g.
Fat-8 g.
Sodium-156 mg.
EXCHANGES: 1/2 skim milk, 1 starch/bread or 1 fruit, 1 fat

Combine gelatin and boiling water, mixing well. Cool slightly. Stir in yogurt and sweetener blending well. Chill in freezer stirring every 5 minutes until very thick but not firm. Combine blueberries and powdered sugar. Fold into gelatin mixture. Pour into graham cracker crust. Chill several hours or until firm. Serve each piece with 1 tablespoon whipped topping, if desired, prepared according to package directions.

Ambrosia Ice Cream Pie

1 8-ounce can unsweetened crushed pineapple
1/4 cup unsweetened shredded coconut
1 teaspoon grated orange rind, if desired
1 package reduced calorie whipped topping mix
2 egg whites
2 tablespoons unsweetened orange juice concentrate
2 tablespoons water
1 teaspoon lemon juice
2 tablespoons sugar
1 packet Equal brand sweetener
1 9-inch baked easy pastry shell (see recipe page 191)

YIELD: 1 pie
SERVING SIZE: 1/8 pie
PER SERVING: Calories-195
Carbohydrate-25 g.
Protein-3 g.
Fat-10 g.
Sodium-114 mg.
EXCHANGES: 1 1/2 starch/bread, 2 fat

Thoroughly drain pineapple. Pat pineapple dry on paper towel. Combine drained pineapple, coconut, and orange rind; set aside. Prepare whipped topping mix as directed on package; refrigerate while preparing filling. In large mixing bowl, combine egg whites, orange juice concentrate, water, lemon juice, and sugar. Using an electric mixer, beat at highest speed until stiff peaks form, 5 to 7 minutes. Gently fold pineapple mixture and sweetener into whipped topping. Very carefully fold whipped topping mixture into egg white mixture using as few strokes as possible. It does not need to be completely blended. Spoon into baked pastry shell. Freeze until firm, 4 to 5 hours. Let thaw 10 to 15 minutes before serving.

Banana Ice Cream Pie

1 package reduced calorie whipped topping mix
2 egg whites
2 tablespoons water
1 teaspoon lemon juice
1 1/2 teaspoons vanilla
2 tablespoons sugar
1 banana, mashed
2 packets Equal brand sweetener
1 9-inch baked easy pastry shell (see recipe page 191)

YIELD: 1 pie
SERVING SIZE: 1/8 pie
PER SERVING: Calories-161
Carbohydrate-18 g.
Protein-3 g.
Fat-9 g.
Sodium-113 mg.
EXCHANGES: 1 starch/bread, 2 fat

Prepare whipped topping mix according to package directions. Refrigerate while preparing filling. In large mixing bowl, combine egg whites, water, lemon juice, vanilla, and sugar. Using an electric mixer, beat at highest speed until soft peaks form; add mashed banana. Continue beating until stiff peaks form. Add sweetener to whipped topping. Very carefully fold whipped topping mixture into egg white mixture using as few strokes as possible; it does not need to be completely blended. Spoon into baked pastry shell. Freeze untl firm, 4 to 5 hours. Let thaw 10 to 15 minutes before serving.

Date Dream Pie

3/4 cup unsweetened chopped dates
1/3 cup water
2 packets Equal brand sweetener
2 tablespoons chopped walnuts
1 package reduced calorie whipped topping mix
2 egg whites
2 tablespoons water
1 teaspoon lemon juice
1 1/2 teaspoons vanilla
2 tablespoons sugar
1 9-inch baked easy pastry shell (see recipe page 191)

YIELD: 1 pie
SERVING SIZE: 1/8 pie
PER SERVING: Calories-190
Carbohydrate-23 g.
Protein-3 g.
Fat-10 g.
Sodium-113 mg.
EXCHANGES: 1 1/2 starch/bread, 2 fat

In small saucepan, combine dates and water; bring to boil. Turn off heat. Cool completely. Add 1 packet sweetener and nuts. Set aside. Prepare whipped topping mix according to package directions. Refrigerate. In large mixing bowl, combine egg whites, water, lemon juice, vanilla, and sugar. Using an electric mixer, beat at highest speed until stiff peaks form, 5 to 7 minutes. Combine date mixture, whipped topping, and the other packet of sweetener. Very carefully fold whipped topping mixture into egg white mixture, using as few strokes as possible; it does not need to be completely blended. Spoon into baked pastry shell. Freeze until firm, 4 to 5 hours. Let thaw 10 to 15 minutes before serving.

THE JOY OF DESSERTS

Must you give up desserts to remain on a healthful diet? No, try these desserts instead! Not only have they been reduced in sugar, but they also have been modified to lower the fat content, especially saturated fats. Fruit is used as a natural sweetener, and it also lends attractiveness to the appearance of of these desserts. Most of these desserts are less than 200 calories per serving. Several of them are even less than 100 calories!

Lemon-Walnut Bundt Cake

2/3 cup margarine
1/2 cup sugar
2 eggs
2 teaspoons grated lemon rind
2 teaspoons vanilla
2 cups plus 1 tablespoon all-purpose flour
1 1/2 teaspoons baking powder
1 teaspoon baking soda
1/2 teaspoon salt
1 cup plain lowfat yogurt
1/3 cup finely chopped walnuts
1 teaspoon powdered sugar

YIELD: 30
SERVING SIZE: 1
PER SERVING: Calories-96
Carbohydrate-10 g.
Protein-2 g.
Fat-5 g.
Sodium-162 mg.
EXCHANGES: 1/2 starch/bread, 1 fat

Thoroughly cream together margarine and sugar. Beat in eggs one at a time until well blended. Add lemon rind and vanilla. Sift flour, baking powder, soda, and salt. Alternately add dry ingredients and yogurt to creamed mixture, beating well after each addition. Fold in chopped walnuts. Spoon batter in well-oiled and floured bundt or tube pan. Bake at 350° for 60 to 65 minutes or until cake tests done. Cool 5 minutes. Remove from pan and cool on wire rack. Sprinkle 1 teaspoon powdered sugar over top. Slice into 30 pieces.

A real prize winner! It's great for coffee parties or brunch.

Pineapple Upside-Down Cake

2 tablespoons margarine
1 tablespoon honey
1 tablespoon brown sugar
1 8-ounce can unsweetened pineapple slices, with juice
1/4 cup margarine
3 tablespoons honey
1 egg
1 teaspoon grated orange rind, if desired
1 1/3 cups all-purpose flour
2 teaspoons baking powder
1/2 teaspoon salt

YIELD: 12
SERVING SIZE: 1
PER SERVING: Calories-139
Carbohydrate-19 g.
Protein-2 g.
Fat-6 g.
Sodium-269 mg.
EXCHANGES: 1 starch/bread, 1 fat

Melt 2 tablespoons margarine in 8 inch square pan. Stir in 1 tablespoon honey and 1 tablespoon brown sugar. Drain pineapple, measuring juice; add enough water to juice to make 1/2 cup of liquid. Place pineapple slices in honey mixture in pan. Set aside. Beat together 1/4 cup margarine and 3 tablespoons honey. Add egg and orange rind. Combine flour, baking powder, and salt. Alternately add dry ingredients and pineapple juice to the margarine mixture, beating well after each addition. Spread over pineapple. Bake at 350° for 30 to 35 minutes or until done. Let stand in pan 3 to 4 minutes, invert pan onto wire rack. Cut into 12 pieces. Serve warm.

Cocoa Banana Nut Dessert

1/2 cup margarine
1/2 cup honey
2 eggs
2 1/2 cups all-purpose flour
1 1/2 teaspoons baking powder
1 teaspoon baking soda
1/2 teaspoon salt
2/3 cup lowfat buttermilk
1 cup mashed, fully ripe bananas (2 bananas)
1 teaspoon vanilla
1/4 cup finely chopped walnuts

Topping:
2 bananas
1 package reduced calorie whipped topping mix
2 tablespoons unsweetened cocoa powder

YIELD: 28
SERVING SIZE: 1
PER SERVING: Calories-109
Carbohydrate-16 g.
Protein-2 g.
Fat-5 g.
Sodium-143 mg.
EXCHANGES: 1 starch/bread, 1 fat

Cream together margarine and honey in large mixing bowl. Add eggs one at a time, beating after each addition. Sift flour, baking powder, soda, and salt. In separate bowl, combine buttermilk, bananas, and vanilla. Alternately add dry ingredients and banana mixture to creamed mixture, mixing thoroughly, beginning and ending with flour. Fold in chopped walnuts. Pour into oiled 9 x 13 inch pan. Bake at 350° for 30 to 35 minutes.

Topping: Slice bananas and place in single layer over top of cake. In chilled mixing bowl, prepare whipped topping mix according to package directions. When topping mix is almost stiff, beat in cocoa powder; continue beating until thick and fluffy. Spread over bananas on cake. Immediately place in refrigerator and chill at least 2 hours.

Date and Chocolate Chip Cake

1 cup chopped unsweetened dates
1 1/2 teaspoons baking soda
1 2/3 cups boiling water
1/2 cup margarine
1/2 cup sugar
2 eggs
1 3/4 cups all-purpose flour
1/2 teaspoon baking soda
1 teaspoon baking powder
1/2 teaspoon salt
3 tablespoons mini semisweet chocolate chips
3 tablespoons finely chopped walnuts

YIELD: 28
SERVING SIZE: 1
PER SERVING: Calories-102
Carbohydrate-12 g.
Protein-2 g.
Fat-6 g.
Sodium-105 mg.
EXCHANGES: 1 starch/bread, 1 fat

Combine dates and 1 1/2 teaspoons soda in small pan. Pour boiling water over dates; stir to blend. Let stand 30 minutes. Cream margarine and sugar. Add eggs and beat well. Combine flour, soda, baking powder, and salt. Alternately add dry ingredients and date mixture to creamed mixture beginning and ending with dry ingredients. Batter will be thin. Pour into oiled and floured 9 x 13 inch baking pan. Sprinkle chocolate chips and walnuts over batter. Bake at 350° for 25 to 30 minutes or until cake tests done. Cool. Cut into 28 pieces (4 across and 7 down).

A dandy of a dessert!

Spicy Pumpkin Torte

1/2 cup chopped unsweetened dates
1/4 cup chopped walnuts
2 tablespoons flour
1/4 cup margarine
1/4 cup honey
2/3 cup cooked pumpkin
1 teaspoon vanilla
2 eggs
1/2 cup all-purpose flour
1 teaspoon baking powder
1 teaspoon pumpkin pie spice
1/4 teaspoon baking soda

YIELD: 8
SERVING SIZE: 1
PER SERVING: Calories-120
Carbohydrate-14 g.
Protein-2 g.
Fat-7 g.
Sodium-146 mg.
EXCHANGES: 1 starch/bread, 1 fat

Combine dates, nuts, and 2 tablespoons flour; set aside. Melt margarine over low heat; stir in honey, blending well. Remove from heat. Add pumpkin and vanilla. Beat in eggs one at a time. Combine dry ingredients and add to pumpkin mixture, mixing thoroughly. Blend in floured dates and nuts. Pour into oiled 9 x 1 1/2 inch round baking pan. Bake at 350° for 20 to 25 minutes until golden brown. Serve warm. If desired serve with 1 tablespoon reduced calorie whipped topping.

A nice addition to a holiday buffet.

Strawberry Delight

2/3 cup graham cracker crumbs
1 1/2 tablespoons sugar
3 tablespoons margarine, melted
4 ounces Neufchâtel cheese
1 tablespoon sugar
1 tablespoon skim milk
1 package reduced calorie whipped topping mix
1 teaspoon sugar
2 cups sliced fresh strawberries
1 package (4-serving size) instant sugar-free vanilla pudding and pie filling mix
1 12-ounce can evaporated skim milk, chilled

YIELD: 10
SERVING SIZE: 1
PER SERVING: Calories-261
Carbohydrate-23 g.
Protein-13 g.
Fat-13 g.
Sodium-210 mg.
EXCHANGES: 1 starch/bread, 1 skim milk, 2 fat

Combine graham cracker crumbs and sugar. Stir in melted margarine. Press in bottom of oiled 6 x 10 inch glass baking dish. Bake at 350° for 5 to 8 minutes. Chill. Beat cheese until smooth; add sugar and milk. Prepare 1 package whipped topping mix according to package directions. Divide in half. Fold half into cheese mixture and spread over pressed graham crackers. Combine 1 teaspoon sugar and strawberries. Spread over cheese. Prepare instant pudding according to directions using the evaporated skim milk. Spread over strawberries; then spread on remaining whipped topping. Chill several hours or overnight. Cut into 10 pieces.

Easy Peanut Butter Cupcakes

1/4 cup peanut butter
3 tablespoons margarine
1 teaspoon vanilla
1/4 cup honey
1 egg
1 cup all-purpose flour
1 teaspoon baking powder
1/4 teaspoon salt
1/3 cup skim milk

YIELD: 10
SERVING SIZE: 1
PER SERVING: Calories-140
Carbohydrate-17 g.
Protein-4 g.
Fat-7 g.
Sodium-159 mg.
EXCHANGES: 1 starch/bread, 1 fat

Blend together peanut butter and margarine. Add vanilla and honey, beating well. Beat in egg. Combine flour, baking powder, and salt. Add to creamed mixture alternately with milk. Place 10 cupcake liners in muffin cups. Fill 1/2 full. Bake at 375° for 15 to 20 minutes or until lightly browned.

Cinnamon Apple Cobbler

1/2 teaspoon cinnamon
3 tablespoons honey
4 cups thinly sliced, peeled baking apples
1/4 cup chopped walnuts
1 cup all-purpose flour
1 teaspoon baking powder
1/4 teaspoon salt
1 egg, beaten
1/3 cup unsweetened apple juice concentrate
2 tablespoons skim milk
1/4 cup margarine, melted

YIELD: 8
SERVING SIZE: 1
PER SERVING: Calories-220
Carbohydrate-37 g.
Protein-2 g.
Fat-8 g.
Sodium-225 mg.
EXCHANGES: 1 starch/bread, 1 fruit, 1 1/2 fat

Mix together cinnamon and honey. Pour over apples, gently stirring until all are coated. Place apples in bottom of oiled 8-inch round baking dish. Sprinkle with 2 tablespoons of nuts. Combine dry ingredients, set aside. Combine egg, apple juice concentrate, milk, and melted margarine; add dry ingredients all at once and mix until smooth. Pour over apples . and sprinkle with remaining nuts. Bake at 325° for 50 to 55 minutes or until done. Cut into 8 pieces. Serve warm. If desired, serve with 1 tablespoon reduced calorie whipped topping.

Baked Apple Snack

4 baking apples, sliced, unpeeled
1/4 cup raisins
3/4 cup quick-cooking rolled oats
1/3 cup all-purpose flour
2 teaspoons cinnamon
1/4 cup water
1/4 cup margarine
1 cup plain lowfat yogurt
2 tablespoons honey

YIELD: 8
SERVING SIZE: 1
PER SERVING: Calories-175
Carbohydrate-28 g.
Protein-3 g.
Fat-7 g.
Sodium-86 mg.
EXCHANGES: 1 fruit, 1 starch/bread

Lay sliced apples in oiled 8-inch square pan. Combine raisins, oats, flour, and cinnamon and sprinkle on top of apples. Sprinkle water over top and dot with margarine. Bake at 350° for 30 to 35 minutes. Spoon into small serving dishes. Mix yogurt and honey, allowing 2 tablespoons per serving. Serves 8.

Baked Apples

6 baking apples, cored
1 1/2 cups water
2 1/4 teaspoons liquid artificial sweetener
1/2 teaspoon cinnamon
6 dates
2 packets Equal brand sweetener

YIELD: 6
SERVING SIZE: 1
PER SERVING: Calories-107
Carbohydrate-28 g.
Protein-trace
Fat-1 g.
Sodium-3 mg.
EXCHANGES: 2 fruit

Pare upper half of apples. Place in shallow baking dish. Combine remaining ingredients except dates and sweetener. Pour over apples. Fill center of each apple with one date. Cover and bake at 350° for 30 minutes. Uncover and bake for an additional 45 to 60 minutes, basting frequently, until apples are tender. After cooking, combine sweetener with juice in pan and baste apples before serving. Serve hot.

Filled Strawberry Crepes

For crepes:
1 cup all-purpose flour
1/4 teaspoon salt
1 tablespoon honey
3 eggs
1 12-ounce can evaporated skim milk

For filling:
1 cup plain lowfat yogurt
1/3 cup low-sugar strawberry spread
2 packets Equal brand sweetener

YIELD: 14
SERVING SIZE: 1
PER SERVING: Calories-93
Carbohydrate-14 g.
Protein-6 g.
Fat-2 g.
Sodium-104 mg.
EXCHANGES: 1 starch/bread

Combine flour and salt. In separate bowl, mix honey, eggs, and milk. Beating with electric mixer on medium speed, gradually add milk mixture to flour mixture until well blended. Heat small (6-inch) teflon coated skillet with several drops of vegetable oil. Make crepes, one at a time, using about 3 tablespoons of batter per crepe, cooking each side about 1 1/2 minutes. Cool slightly. For filling, thoroughly combine yogurt, strawberry spread, and sweetener. Fill each crepe with 1 1/2 tablespoons of strawberry crepe filling. Roll up jelly roll style.
Serve warm.

These make a hit with any age. Great for parties or brunch.

Cherry-Pineapple Compote

1 20-ounce can unsweetened pineapple tidbits
1 16-ounce can unsweetened pears, drained
1 orange, peeled and chopped
1 teaspoon grated orange rind
1/4 cup unsweetened orange juice concentrate
1/2 cup water
1 tablespoon honey
1 16 1/2-ounce can pitted dark cherries, well drained

YIELD: 4 cups
SERVING SIZE: 1/2 cup
PER SERVING: Calories-156
Carbohydrate-38 g.
Protein-1 g.
Fat-none
Sodium-trace
EXCHANGES: 2 1/2 fruit

Drain pineapple, reserving 2/3 cup juice. Slice pears; add pears and chopped orange to pineapple tidbits. Combine reserved pineapple juice, orange rind, orange juice concentrate, water, and honey. Arrange fruits in shallow baking dish. Pour juice mixture over fruits. Bake at 325° for 15 minutes. Thoroughly rinse dark cherries. Add cherries to fruit mixture and bake 10 more minutes and serve warm.

Variation: After fruit mixture has baked for 15 minutes, substitute 2 sliced bananas for dark cherries. Do not bake the additional 10 minutes.

A delightful after-dinner fruit dessert.

Blueberry Pudding

1 1/2 cups fresh or unsweetened frozen blueberries
2 tablespoons all-purpose flour
1 tablespoon grated lemon rind
1 teaspoon sugar
1 egg
1/4 cup honey
2 tablespoons margarine
2 teaspoons vanilla
1 1/2 cups all-purpose flour
2 teaspoons baking powder
1/4 teaspoon salt
3/4 cup warm skim milk

Hard Sauce:
1/3 cup light cream cheese
1 teaspoon lemon juice
1/2 teaspoon grated lemon rind
2 teaspoons honey

YIELD: 16
SERVING SIZE: 1
PER SERVING: Calories-102
Carbohydrate-16 g.
Protein-2 g.
Fat-3 g.
Sodium-136 mg.
EXCHANGES: 1 starch/bread, 1/2 fat

If using frozen blueberries, thoroughly thaw and drain; pat dry with paper towel. In small bowl, combine blueberries, 2 tablespoons flour, lemon rind, and sugar. Set aside. Beat together egg, honey, margarine, and vanilla until light and fluffy. Combine flour, baking powder, and salt. Alternately add dry ingredients and warm milk to creamed mixture, beginning and ending with dry ingredients. Gently fold in blueberry mixture. Pour into a well-oiled and floured 6-cup ring mold. Bake at 350° for 30 to 35 minutes or until lightly brown and wooden toothpick inserted in center comes out clean. Cool pudding in mold for 5 minutes, then remove to wire rack. Serve pudding warm with hard sauce.

For sauce, combine cream cheese, lemon juice, grated lemon rind, and honey. Spread over top of warm blueberry pudding. Cut into 16 slices.

Fruit Filled Melon

1 egg, slightly beaten
1 1/2 tablespoons honey
1 teaspoon grated orange rind
1/3 cup orange juice
1/3 cup plain lowfat yogurt
1 medium cantaloupe
1 cup sliced fresh strawberries
1 cup fresh blueberries

YIELD: 4
SERVING SIZE: 1
PER SERVING: Calories-153
Carbohydrate-32 g.
Protein-5 g.
Fat-2 g.
Sodium-51 mg.
EXCHANGES: 2 fruit

Prepare honey dressing by stirring together egg, honey, orange rind, and orange juice in small pan over low heat. Stir constantly until thickened, 6 to 8 minutes. Remove from heat. Refrigerate, covered, until well chilled. Fold into yogurt. Cut cantaloupe into quarters, scoop out seeds. Fold strawberries and blueberries into dressing. Divide fruit mixture among cantaloupe quarters. Serve immediately.

A cool, refreshing summertime dessert.

Applesauce Fruit Gelatin

1 1/4 cups unsweetened applesauce
1 package sugar-free strawberry flavored gelatin
3/4 cup sugar-free lemon-lime carbonated beverage
1/2 cup sliced fresh fruit, such as strawberries or apples

YIELD: 2 1/2 cups
SERVING SIZE: 1/2 cup
PER SERVING: Calories-39
Carbohydrate-7 g.
Protein-1 g.
Fat-trace
Sodium-48 mg.
EXCHANGES: 1/2 fruit

Heat applesauce over medium heat until bubbly. Remove from heat. Add gelatin, stirring to dissolve. Stir in carbonated beverage, then fresh fruit. Pour into small flat dish or 5 foil-lined muffin cups. Chill until firm.

Gelatin Soufflé

1 cup evaporated skim milk, chilled
1/2 cup unsweetened orange juice concentrate
1 cup water
1 package sugar-free lime flavored gelatin

YIELD: 6
SERVING SIZE: 1
PER SERVING: Calories-44
Carbohydrate-7 g.
Protein-4 g.
Fat-trace
Sodium-93 mg.
EXCHANGES: 1/2 fruit

Chill a medium sized mixing bowl and beaters. Thoroughly chill the evaporated milk. In saucepan, combine orange juice concentrate and water; bring to a boil. Reduce heat and add gelatin. Stir constantly until gelatin is dissolved. Remove from heat. Chill in freezer until gelatin begins to set, about 10 minutes, stirring often. In chilled mixing bowl, beat chilled evaporated milk with electric mixer at highest speed until milk is very stiff and peaks form. Immediately fold into chilled gelatin. Gently spoon into 6 cups or small bowls. Chill several hours before serving.

Orange Whip

2 packages unflavored gelatin
1 cup boiling water
1 cup orange juice
1 cup plain lowfat yogurt
3 to 4 packets Equal brand sweetener
1 orange, sliced

YIELD: 3 cups
SERVING SIZE: 1/2 cup
PER SERVING: Calories-37
Carbohydrate-7 g.
Protein-4 g.
Fat-1 g.
Sodium-21 mg.
EXCHANGES: 1/2 fruit

Dissolve gelatin in boiling water. Add orange juice. Chill until almost set. Beat until fluffy. Fold in yogurt. Add sweetener to taste. Pour into individual serving dishes. Garnish with fresh orange slice.

Chocolate Smunchies

1 package sugar-free chocolate pudding mix
2 cups skim milk
3 cups peanut butter
70 graham cracker squares
1 envelope reduced calorie whipped topping mix

YIELD: 35
SERVING SIZE: 1
PER SERVING: Calories-200
Carbohydrate-17 g.
Protein-8 g.
Fat-12 g.
Sodium-142 mg.
EXCHANGES: 1 starch/bread,
1 medium-fat meat, 1 fat

Mix chocolate pudding according to directions on package, using skim milk. Cool thoroughly. Mix peanut butter with pudding. Drop 2 tablespoons onto each graham cracker square. Place 1 tablespoon whipped topping on top of the pudding-peanut butter mixture and cover with second graham cracker square to make a sandwich. Wrap and freeze.

Banana Smunchies

2 cups ripe bananas, mashed (4 bananas)
2 cups peanut butter
52 graham cracker squares

YIELD: 26
SERVING SIZE: 1
PER SERVING: Calories-188
Carbohydrate-20 g.
Protein-7 g.
Fat-11 g.
Sodium-118 mg.
EXCHANGES: 1 starch/bread, 1 medium-fat meat, 1 fat

Combine bananas with peanut butter. Chill well. Drop 2 tablespoons onto a graham cracker square, cover with second graham cracker square. Wrap and freeze.

THE JOY OF SWEET TIDBITS

Here are recipes to satisfy even the strongest of sweet cravings. Even though some of these recipes contain sugar and/or honey, the amount has been greatly reduced compared with regular candy. Store these tidbits in airtight containers. Many can be successfully frozen for later use.

As-Good-As Fudge

1/2 cup honey
1/2 cup peanut butter
1/2 cup cocoa powder
3/4 cup sunflower seeds
1/4 cup unsweetened shredded coconut
1/2 cup chopped unsweetened dates
1/3 cup chopped walnuts
1/4 cup sesame seeds

YIELD: 36
SERVING SIZE: 1
PER SERVING: Calories–77
Carbohydrate–7 g.
Protein–3 g.
Fat–5 g.
Sodium–25 mg.
EXCHANGES: 1/2 starch/bread, 1 fat

In small pan over low heat, stir together honey and peanut butter until smooth. Remove from heat; add cocoa powder and blend well. Add remaining ingredients. Press into oiled 9 x 9 x 2-inch pan. Cut into 36 squares. Chill until firm.

230.

Crunchy Cocoa Chews

1 cup peanut butter
1/2 cup honey
1/4 cup instant nonfat dry milk powder
1/4 cup cocoa powder
1/2 cup raisins
1/4 cup wheat germ
1/4 cup unsweetened shredded coconut
1 cup sunflower seeds

YIELD: 36
SERVING SIZE: 1
PER SERVING: Calories–91
Carbohydrate–9 g.
Protein–4 g.
Fat–5 g.
Sodium–14 mg.
EXCHANGES: 1/2 starch/bread, 1 fat

Combine peanut butter and honey. Add dry milk powder and cocoa powder. Stir in raisins, wheat germ, and coconut. Form into 36 small balls. Roll in sunflower seeds. Chill.

Grinder Snacks

2/3 cup raisins
2/3 cup figs (about 8)
2/3 cup dates
1/8 teaspoon lemon juice
2 tablespoons graham cracker crumbs

YIELD: 16
SERVING SIZE: 1
PER SERVING: Calories-60
Carbohydrate-15 g.
Fat-trace
Sodium-7 mg.
EXCHANGES: 1 fruit

Grind together raisins, figs, and dates. Add lemon juice to cracker crumbs. Roll one rounded teaspoon of fruit mixture into a ball. Roll ball in cracker crumbs until coated. Store in airtight container.

Peanut Nuggets

2 eggs
1 1/3 cups graham cracker crumbs
1/4 cup chunky peanut butter
1 tablespoon honey
2 teaspoons baking powder
1/4 teaspoon salt
1 tablespoon skim milk

YIELD: 24
SERVING SIZE: 3
PER SERVING: Calories-135
Carbohydrate-15 g.
Protein-3 g.
Fat-6 g.
Sodium-297 mg.
EXCHANGES: 1 starch/bread, 1 fat

Beat eggs in small mixing bowl until thick and lemon colored. Add graham cracker crumbs, peanut butter, honey, baking powder, and salt. Blend well. Stir in milk. Drop by small teaspoonfuls onto ungreased baking sheet. Bake at 350° for 8 to 10 minutes.

Peanut Butter Crunchies

3/4 cup chunky peanut butter
2 tablespoons honey
3/4 cup corn flake crumbs

YIELD: 24
SERVING SIZE: 1
PER SERVING: Calories–79
Carbohydrate–9 g.
Protein–3 g.
Fat–4 g.
Sodium–116 mg.
EXCHANGES: 1/2 starch/bread, 1 fat

Thoroughly blend peanut butter and honey. Stir in 1/2 cup corn flake crumbs. Form into 24 small balls and roll in remaining corn flake crumbs. Chill.

For peanut butter lovers!

Peanut Butter Crunchies II

3/4 cup chunky peanut butter
2 tablespoons honey
3/4 cup Grape-Nuts brand cereal

YIELD: 24
SERVING SIZE: 1
PER SERVING: Calories-64
Carbohydrate-6 g.
Protein-3 g.
Fat-4 g.
Sodium-64 mg.
EXCHANGES: 1/2 starch/bread, 1 fat

Mix 1/2 cup cereal with peanut butter and honey. Form into 24 small balls and roll in remaining cereal. Chill.

A crunchy variation.

235.

Sunflower and Sesame Squares

1/2 cup honey
1/2 cup peanut butter
3/4 cup instant nonfat dry milk powder
3/4 cup sesame seeds
3/4 cup sunflower seeds

YIELD: 36
SERVING SIZE: 1
PER SERVING: Calories–93
Carbohydrate–7 g.
Protein–5 g.
Fat–5 g.
Sodium–39 mg.
EXCHANGES: 1/2 starch/bread, 1 fat

In small pan over low heat, stir together honey and peanut butter until smooth. Remove from heat and add remaining ingredients. Press into oiled 8 x 8 x 2-inch pan. Bake at 325° for 12 to 15 minutes or until slightly brown. Do not overbake. Mixture will still be soft. Immediately cut into 36 squares. Refrigerate 2 to 3 hours or until hard.

Almost like candy!

Health Snack

1/2 cup creamy peanut butter
2 1/2 tablespoons carob powder
1 small banana, mashed (about 1/3 cup)
1 1/2 teaspoons honey
1/4 cup finely chopped walnuts

YIELD: 16
SERVING SIZE: 2
PER SERVING: Calories–96
Carbohydrate–10 g.
Protein–2 g.
Fat–6 g.
Sodium–40 mg.
EXCHANGES: 1 fruit, 1 fat

Thoroughly combine first four ingredients (an electric mixer works best). Form into 16 small balls and roll in chopped walnuts. Store in refrigerator.

As good tasting as it is good for you.

Banana Chips

4 small bananas
1/4 cup lemon juice

YIELD: 4 servings
SERVING SIZE: 1/4 recipe
PER SERVING: Calories-85
Carbohydrate-22 g.
Protein-1 g.
Fat-trace
Sodium-1 mg.
EXCHANGES: 1 1/2 fruit

Slice bananas and dip into lemon juice. Place on oiled baking sheet in a single layer. Bake at 175° for 2 to 3 hours, until golden. Store in airtight container.

An easy-to-make delightful snack.

Fruit and Nut Gems

1/3 cup chopped dry roasted peanuts, unsalted
1/3 cup chopped walnuts
1/3 cup slivered almonds
1/3 cup roasted sunflower seeds, unsalted
1/3 cup raisins
1/3 cup unsweetened shredded coconut
1/3 cup quick-cooking rolled oats
1/3 cup chopped, unsweetened dates
3 tablespoons honey
1/4 cup peanut butter
1 teaspoon vanilla

YIELD: 30
SERVING SIZE: 1
PER SERVING: Calories–80
Carbohydrate–6 g.
Protein–3 g.
Fat–6 g.
Sodium–16 mg.
EXCHANGES: 1/2 fruit, 1 fat

Thoroughly combine all ingredients. Shape into 30 balls by pressing a small amount of the nut mixture into a teaspoon. Transfer to foil or waxed paper lined tray. Freeze. Serve frozen.

Energy Treats

2 tablespoons honey
1/2 cup chunky peanut butter
1/3 cup raisins
1/3 cup instant nonfat dry milk powder
1/4 cup crisp rice cereal
1/3 cup crushed pretzel sticks

YIELD: 24
SERVING SIZE: 2
PER SERVING: Calories–92
Carbohydrate–14 g.
Protein–4 g.
Fat–2 g.
Sodium–152 mg.
EXCHANGES: 1 starch/bread

Mix together honey and peanut butter; add raisins and dry milk. Stir in rice cereal. Form into 24 small balls. Roll in pretzel crumbs. Store in refrigerator.

THE JOY OF FROZEN SNACKS

Many of the commercial reduced-calorie frozen snacks contain sweeteners, such as sorbitol, that cause a grainy, unpleasant texture. The frozen snacks in this section are not grainy if you follow the directions carefully. The sweetness in these recipes comes from fruits, fruit juices, sugar-free fruit-flavored carbonated beverages, and sugar-free fruit-flavored gelatin. Vanilla also enhances the sweetness of foods made with less sugar. Evaporated skim milk and plain lowfat yogurt replace higher fat dairy products.

To make your frozen snacks a success, use chilled ingredients during preparation and store the snacks in the coldest part of your freezer. When possible, freeze in individual serving dishes and thaw at room temperature for 10 to 15 minutes before serving.

Fruity Ice Cream

1 package (1 1/2 ounces) reduced calorie whipped topping mix
1 egg, separated
3 packets Equal brand sweetener
1 teaspoon vanilla
1 cup finely diced fresh fruit, such as strawberries, peaches, or blueberries

YIELD: 6
SERVING SIZE: 1
PER SERVING: Calories–24
Carbohydrate–3 g.
Protein–trace
Fat–1 g.
Sodium–2 mg.
EXCHANGES: free

Prepare whipped topping according to package directions. When topping is stiff, beat in egg yolk and sweetener. Beat egg white until stiff peaks form. Gently fold into whipped topping. Freeze for 1/2 hour, then beat again. Fold in fresh fruit and pour into 1-quart refrigerator tray or 6 foil-lined muffin cups. Freeze until firm.

Cranberry Sherbet

1 package sugar-free strawberry flavored gelatin
1 cup boiling low-calorie cranberry juice cocktail
2 cups cold low-calorie cranberry juice cocktail
1 cup evaporated skim milk
3 packets Equal brand sweetener
1/2 cup finely sliced fresh strawberries

YIELD: 4 1/2 cups
SERVING SIZE: 1 cup
PER SERVING: Calories-80
Carbohydrate-14 g.
Protein-4 g.
Fat-trace
Sodium-76 mg.
EXCHANGES: 1 starch/bread or 1 fruit

Pour gelatin into boiling cranberry juice, stirring until dissolved. Stir in cold cranberry juice. Beat in evaporated milk and 2 packets sweetener. Mix 1 packet sweetener with strawberries and gently stir into cranberry mixture. Freeze in shallow pan, stirring occasionally until mixture is frozen but slightly mushy, 1 1/2 to 2 hours. Serve sherbet slightly soft.

Raspberry Sherbet

1 12-ounce can sugar-free ginger ale
1/2 cup nonfat dry milk powder
3/4 teaspoon liquid artificial sweetener, if desired
1 1/2 cups fresh raspberries
1/4 teaspoon vanilla

YIELD: 3 1/2 cups
SERVING SIZE: 1/2 cup
PER SERVING: Calories-30
Carbohydrate-5 g.
Protein-2 g.
Fat-trace
Sodium-40 mg.
EXCHANGES: 1/2 fruit

Whirl all ingredients in blender until smooth. Freeze until mixture reaches consistency of soft sherbet. (Note: Can also be made with strawberries and sugar-free strawberry soda instead of raspberries and ginger ale.)

246.

Strawberry Ice

4 cups fresh strawberries, sliced
1 1/2 teaspoons lemon juice
1 tablespoon honey

YIELD: 2 1/2 cups
SERVING SIZE: 1/2 cup
PER SERVING: Calories-67
Carbohydrate-16 g.
Protein-1 g.
Fat-trace
Sodium-trace
EXCHANGES: 1 fruit

Whirl all ingredients in food processor or blender until smooth. Pour into shallow pan. Cover and freeze until solid. Remove from freezer and blend until slushy. Pour into bowl, cover, and freeze. Soften slightly before spooning into serving dishes.

Frosty Strawberry "Cupcakes"

1 cup plain lowfat yogurt
1/2 cup unsweetened frozen strawberries, thawed
1 8-ounce can unsweetened crushed pineapple, undrained
1/4 cup unsweetened apple juice concentrate

YIELD: 12
SERVING SIZE: 1
PER SERVING: Calories-30
Carbohydrate-8 g.
Protein-1 g.
Fat-trace
Sodium-39 mg.
EXCHANGES: 1/2 fruit

Whirl all ingredients in blender until smooth. Pour into 12 foil or paper-lined muffin cups. Freeze until solid. Thaw at least 15 minutes before serving.

Frozen Fruit Delight

1 cup sugar-free lemon-lime carbonated beverage
1 large banana, sliced
1/2 cup unsweetened orange juice concentrate
1 8-ounce can unsweetened crushed pineapple, undrained
1 cup unsweetened frozen strawberries, thawed and undrained
1 teaspoon lemon juice

YIELD: 13
SERVING SIZE: 1
PER SERVING: Calories-38
Carbohydrate-7 g.
Protein-trace
Fat-trace
Sodium-24 mg.
EXCHANGES: 1/2 fruit

Combine all ingredients in large bowl, stirring to blend well. Spoon into 13 foil-lined muffin cups allowing 1/3 cup per serving. Freeze until firm. Thaw at least 15 minutes before serving.

249.

Pineapple Yogurt Freeze

1 8-ounce can unsweetened crushed pineapple, undrained
1 cup plain lowfat yogurt
1 teaspoon vanilla
2 packets Equal brand sweetener

YIELD: 2 cups
SERVING SIZE: 1/2 cup
PER SERVING: Calories-76
Carbohydrate-14 g.
Protein-3 g.
Fat-1 g.
Sodium-116 mg.
EXCHANGES: 1 starch/bread

Stir all ingredients together and place in shallow pan. Freeze, stirring occasionally until mixture is thick, 20 to 30 minutes. Divide into 4 small bowls. Serve immediately.

Strawberry Freeze

2 egg whites
1 12-ounce can evaporated skim milk
1 12-ounce can sugar-free strawberry flavored carbonated beverage
5 packets Equal brand sweetener
1 cup unsweetened frozen strawberries, thawed and undrained

YIELD: 5 cups
SERVING SIZE: 1 cup
PER SERVING: Calories-100
Carbohydrate-4 g.
Protein-8 g.
Fat-8 g.
Sodium-124 mg.
EXCHANGES: 1/2 skim milk, 1 fat

In small mixing bowl, slightly beat egg whites. Add milk, carbonated beverage, and sweetener, beating well. Stir in strawberries. Pour into two 1-quart refrigerator trays or two 1-quart pans. Freeze, stirring occasionally, until mixture is frozen but slightly mushy, 1 1/2 to 2 hours. Serve slightly soft.

Fruit Fantasy Frozen Cups

5 ounces unsweetened frozen strawberries, thawed
6 tablespoons unsweetened frozen orange juice concentrate, thawed
1 8-ounce can unsweetened crushed pineapple
5 ounces mandarin oranges
2 tablespoons lemon juice
2 bananas, diced

YIELD: 6 1/2 cups
SERVING SIZE: 1/2 cup
PER SERVING: Calories-65
Carbohydrate-13 g.
Protein-1 g.
Fat-trace
Sodium-trace
EXCHANGES: 1 fruit

Thaw strawberries and orange juice. Do not drain fruits. Combine all ingredients in a large bowl. Spoon into paper cups or serving dishes. Freeze until firm. Store in freezer in plastic freezer bags.

Orange–Banana Push–ups

2 bananas
1 6–ounce can orange juice concentrate, thawed
1/2 cup nonfat dry milk powder
1/2 cup water
1 cup plain lowfat yogurt

YIELD: 8
SERVING SIZE: 1
PER SERVING: Calories–120
Carbohydrate–21 g.
Protein–4 g.
Fat–1 g.
Sodium–59 mg.
EXCHANGES: 1/2 skim milk, 1 fruit

Dice bananas. Whirl all ingredients in blender until foamy. Pour into 3 1/2 ounce plastic or paper cups and freeze.

Triple Fruit Freeze

2 tablespoons sugar-free cherry flavored gelatin
2 cups unsweetened orange juice
2 cups mashed bananas (4 large bananas)
1 cup unsweetened crushed pineapple, undrained
2 tablespoons lemon juice
10 pitted cherries, chopped

YIELD: 8 cups
SERVING SIZE: 1/2 cup
PER SERVING: Calories-54
Carbohydrate-13 g.
Protein-2 g.
Fat-trace
Sodium-3 mg.
EXCHANGES: 1 fruit

Combine gelatin powder and orange juice in a saucepan; bring to a boil over medium heat, stirring constantly to dissolve gelatin. Remove from heat and cool for 5 minutes. Combine the mashed bananas, pineapple with juice, lemon juice, and chopped cherries in a 4-quart ice cream freezer. Add the cooled gelatin mixture. Stir until thoroughly mixed. Process according to ice cream freezer instructions (about 30 to 45 minutes).

Pineapple Sherbet Cups

1 8-ounce can unsweetened crushed pineapple
6 packets Equal brand sweetener
1 tablespoon lemon juice
1/2 teaspoon vanilla
1 cup skim milk
popsicle sticks

YIELD: 3 1/2 cups
SERVING SIZE: 1/2 cup
PER SERVING: Calories-38
Carbohydrate-8 g.
Protein-1 g.
Fat-trace
Sodium-18 mg.
EXCHANGES: 1/2 fruit

Drain pineapple, reserving juice. Add water to juice to make 1 cup of liquid. Put mixing bowl, beaters, and drained pineapple in refrigerator to chill. Add sweetener, lemon juice, and vanilla to pineapple juice. Stir until dissolved. Stir gradually into milk. Pour into a 9-inch square pan and freeze until firm around the edges and slushy in the middle.

Spoon this sherbet mixture into mixing bowl and break up with fork; beat slowly until just fluffy. Fold in pineapple. Spoon into plastic or paper cups. Freeze until firm enough to insert sticks. Store in freezer in plastic freezer bags.

255.

Frosted Berry Whip

1 cup berries, fresh or frozen without sugar, thawed
4 unsweetened canned peach halves
2 packets Equal brand sweetener
1 tablespoon lemon juice
popsicle sticks

YIELD: 6
SERVING SIZE: 1 cup
PER SERVING: Calories-28
Carbohydrate-7 g.
Protein-1 g.
Fat-trace
Sodium-trace
EXCHANGES: 1/2 fruit

Place all ingredients in blender, whirl until smooth. Spoon mixture into six 3 1/2 ounce plastic or paper cups and partially freeze. Insert sticks and freeze until firm. Store in freezer in plastic freezer bags.

Berry Slush

1 cup water
12 packets Equal brand sweetener
2 cups orange juice or apricot nectar
1 8-ounce can unsweetened crushed pineapple
1 10-ounce package unsweetened frozen strawberries or raspberries, thawed
1 banana, diced
popsicle sticks

YIELD: 10
SERVING SIZE: 1
PER SERVING: Calories-67
Carbohydrate-15 g.
Protein-1 g.
Fat-trace
Sodium-trace
EXCHANGES: 1 fruit

Heat water, allow to cool slightly. Add sweetener, stir to dissolve. Stir in orange juice or apricot nectar, pineapple, berries, and diced banana. Mix well. Freeze in 3 1/2 ounce plastic or paper cups. When firm enough, insert sticks and freeze until solid. Store in freezer in plastic freezer bags.

Pudding Pops

1 package (4-serving size) reduced calorie pudding mix (not instant)
2 cups skim milk
2/3 cup evaporated skim milk, chilled
3 packets Equal brand sweetener
popsicle sticks

YIELD: 4 1/2 cups
SERVING SIZE: 1/2 cup
PER SERVING: Calories-67
Carbohydrate-8 g.
Protein-5 g.
Fat-2 g.
Sodium-109 mg.
EXCHANGES: 1/2 skim milk

To whip evaporated milk, place the can in refrigerator for several hours or in freezer for one hour before beginning recipe. Chill small mixing bowl and beaters in freezer. In medium size saucepan, combine pudding mix and skim milk. Stir completely to blend. Heat, stirring constantly until pudding bubbles. Turn off heat. Chill pudding in freezer until almost thickened, about 20 minutes, stirring often. Remove from freezer. Beat chilled evaporated milk in chilled mixing bowl at high speed until thick and stiff. Beat in sweetener. Gently fold into pudding mix until well blended. Chill in freezer until pudding near edge of pan is frozen, about 30 minutes. Whip with wire whisk or wooden spoon. Place 9 paper cups in pan. Pour 1/2 cup pudding mix into each cup. Freeze until center is firm enough to hold sticks. Insert sticks and freeze solid. To serve, peel off paper cups.

258.

Banana-Orange Freezer Pops

1 16-ounce can frozen orange juice concentrate, thawed
3 ripe bananas, mashed
1 cup water
popsicle sticks

YIELD: 12
SERVING SIZE: 1
PER SERVING: Calories-54
Carbohydrate-13 g.
Protein-1 g.
Fat-trace
Sodium-trace
EXCHANGES: 1 fruit

Place orange juice, mashed bananas, and water in blender and whirl until smooth. Pour into twelve 3 1/2 ounce paper cups. Freeze 1 hour, then insert sticks and continue to freeze until solid.

259.

Strawberry YoJell Pops

1 package sugar-free strawberry flavored gelatin
1 cup boiling water
1/2 cup cold water
1 cup plain lowfat yogurt
1/2 cup unsweetened frozen strawberries, thawed and drained, or 1/2 cup sliced fresh strawberries
1 packet Equal brand sweetener
popsicle sticks

YIELD: 6
SERVING SIZE: 1
PER SERVING: Calories-30
Carbohydrate-4 g.
Protein-2 g.
Fat-1 g.
Sodium-31 mg.
EXCHANGES: 1/2 fruit

Add gelatin to boiling water, stirring until dissolved. Stir in cold water, then yogurt, strawberries, and sweetener. Mix until well blended. Place 6 paper cups in small pan. Pour 1/2 cup of strawberry mixture into each cup. Freeze until center is firm enough to hold stick, 20 to 30 minutes. Insert stick in center of each cup. Freeze solid. To serve, peel off paper cup.

Fruit Yogurt Popsicles

2 teaspoons unflavored gelatin
3 tablespoons cold water
2 bananas
2 cups fresh strawberries
1 1/2 cups unsweetened orange juice
1 cup plain lowfat yogurt
popsicle sticks

YIELD: 9
SERVING SIZE: 1
PER SERVING: Calories–71
Carbohydrate–15 g.
Protein–2 g.
Fat–trace
Sodium–19 mg.
EXCHANGES: 1 fruit or 1 starch/bread

Soak gelatin in cold water for 3 minutes. Whirl all ingredients except yogurt in blender until smooth. Remove from blender and stir in yogurt. Pour into 3 1/2 ounce plastic or paper cups. Insert sticks and freeze.

261.
THE JOY OF CONVENIENCE SNACK FOODS

There are times when the hustle and bustle of our lives require that we use convenience foods. Convenience foods give us quick, easy to prepare, good tasting, and usually inexpensive snacks. Unfortunately, they do not always provide good nutrition. Many commercial snacks contain significant amounts of fat, salt, sugar, and calories.

By reading the labels of convenience foods, you can make wise choices for snacks. Pay special attention to the list of ingredients. Ingredients are listed in descending order of amount by weight; in other words, the first ingredient is present in the largest amount, and the last ingredient is present in the smallest amount. As you examine the ingredient list of a product, note the order of ingredients and the kinds of ingredients you may want to limit or avoid.

Ingredients to Limit or Avoid

High Saturated Fat Ingredients:

animal fat
lard
meat fat
chicken fat
turkey fat
lamb fat
beef fat
pork fat
bacon fat
cocoa butter
shortening
vegetable shortening

vegetable oil*
palm or palm kernel oil
coconut oil
coconut
vegetable fat*
hardened fat or oil
hydrogenated fat or oil
milk chocolate
butter
whole milk solids
cream and cream sauces
egg and egg yolk solids
*Usually palm or coconut oil

High Sodium Ingredients:

salt (sodium chloride)
monosodium glutamate
broth

bouillon cubes or granules
baking soda
soy sauce

Sources of Sugar:

sucrose
dextrose
fructose
invert sugar
molasses

brown sugar
corn syrup
honey
maple syrup

Acceptable Ingredients

cocoa
safflower oil
sunflower oil
cottonseed oil
corn oil

sesame oil
soybean oil
monoglycerides
diglycerides
nonfat dry milk or solids

In addition to the ingredient list, many labels provide nutrition information per serving. This information will also be of help to you when evaluating food products for fat, sodium, and sugar content. Here is the format currently used for nutrition labeling:

Nutrition Information Per Serving

Serving size	1 oz
Servings per container	6
Calories	130
Protein	3 g
Carbohydrate	18 g
Fat	7 g
Sodium	190 mg

Percentage of U.S. Recommended Daily Allowances (U.S. RDA)

Protein	6
Vitamin A	*
Vitamin C	2
Thiamin	6
Riboflavin	*
Niacin	4
Calcium	*
Iron	6

*Contains less than 2% of the U.S. RDA for these nutrients

Total amount of calories furnished by one serving of food as it comes from the container.

As of 1986, the milligrams of sodium in the serving size is required on products with nutrition labeling.

Percentages of 8 important nutrients supplied by one serving of food as it comes from the container

The amount of food for which nutrition information is given and the number of servings in the container.

Amounts of protein, carbohydrate, and fat (in grams) supplied by one serving of food. One gram of carbohydrate or protein provides 4 calories, one gram of fat provides 9 calories.

Below is an example of nutrition labeling for a specific food product:

Granola Bars

Nutrition Information
Per Serving

Serving size	1 bar (1 oz)
Servings per container	8
Calories	135
Protein	2 g
Carbohydrate	20 g
Fat	5 g
Sodium	90 mg

Percentage of
U.S. Recommended Daily
Allowances (U.S. RDA)

Protein	2
Vitamin A	*
Vitamin C	*
Thiamin	6
Riboflavin	2
Niacin	*
Calcium	*
Iron	2

*Contains less than 2% of the U.S. RDA for these nutrients.

Other food labeling regulations that can help you in evaluating food products are:

- Foods labeled "low calorie" must contain no more than 40 calories per serving; however, a food naturally low in calories cannot be labeled this way.
- Foods labeled "reduced calorie" must be at least one-third lower in calories than the products they are intended to replace.
- "Imitation" foods are synthetic food products made to resemble natural foods, but they may not be nutritionally equal. This does not mean that imitation foods are not acceptable to use. For example, many imitation foods are especially made to be lower in fat and may

be better to use than the original food product. However, it is still wise to read the ingredient listing and the nutrition information on the labels of imitation products.

Many commercial products are advertised and labeled as "diet," "dietary," or "dietetic." In order to be labeled in this way, one ingredient must have been reduced, eliminated, or substituted for another ingredient. These products are not necessarily low-calorie foods, and they are not always useful for people with diabetes, so if you choose to use them, be careful. Since dietetic foods must comply with nutrition labeling regulations, you can use the information on the label to decide if a certain product fits your nutritional needs. Look at the list of ingredients, number of calories, comparative cost, and consider the taste of the product before including it in your diet. Foods labeled "light" or "lite" also have no standard meaning and should be evaluated carefully.

Below is a list of popular convenience snack foods. The exchange value per serving is also provided. These are simply examples of commercial foods that you may wish to use. However, we do not necessarily endorse these products over other, similar products. An asterisk (*) indicates that the item is higher in sugar, fat, and/or sodium content than many other snack foods. People with diabetes or cardiovascular disease should use these items only on an occasional basis.

Convenience Snack Foods

Alba '66 or Alba '77	1 envelope = 1 skim milk or 1 starch
*Chocolate skim milk	1 cup = 1 skim milk, 1 starch, 1/2 fat
Carnation Sugar Free Hot Cocoa Mix	1 envelope = 1/2 skim milk
Swiss Miss Sugar Free Hot Cocoa Mix	1 envelope = 1/2 skim milk
Ovaltine's Sugar Free Hot Cocoa Mix	1 envelope = 1/2 starch
*D-ZERTA brand Reduced Calorie pudding mix made with skim milk	1/2 cup = 1 skim milk or 1 starch
JELL-O brand Sugar Free Pudding	1/2 cup = 1 skim milk or 1 bread

Fruit Corners Fruit Roll-ups	1 = 1 fruit
Fruit Corners Fruit Bars	1 = 1 1/2 fruit
Sunkist Fruit Rolls	1 = 1 fruit
Sunkist Fun Fruits	1 pouch = 1 1/2 fruit
Dried fruit	1/4 cup (1/2 ounce) = 1 fruit
Weight Watchers Apple Snack or Fruit Snack	1 package (1/2 ounce) = 1 fruit
*JELL-O brand Gelatin Pops	1 = 1/2 fruit
Muffin prepared from mix, 1/12 mix (plain, blueberry, or bran)	1 = 1 starch, 1 fat
Bread sticks	
8″ long, 1/2″ diameter	2 = 1 starch
4″ long, 1/4″ diameter	6 = 1 starch
Trail mix (raisin, nut, coconut, fruit mix)	1/4 cup = 1 starch, 1 fat
Animal crackers	8 = 1 starch
Graham crackers, 2 1/2 inches square	3 = 1 starch
*Potato chips	15 or 1 ounce = 1 starch, 2 fat
Pretzels	3/4 ounce = 1 starch
Popcorn, popped with no fat added	3 cups popped = 1 starch
*Ginger snaps	3 = 1 starch
Vanilla Wafers	6 = 1 starch, 1 fat
*Frozen Fruit Yogurt	1/3 cup = 1 starch
*Granola Bar (not dipped or coated)	1 small = 1 starch, 1 fat
*JELL-O brand Pudding Pop	1 = 1 starch, 1/2 fat
*Nuts or seeds (peanuts, sunflower seeds, etc.)	1/4 cup = 1 medium fat meat, 2 fat

Source: *Convenience Food Facts*, International Diabetes Center, 1984

Appendix

What are the Exchange Lists?

A widely used guide to meal planning for people with diabetes and anyone interested in a healthful diet is the *Exchange Lists for Meal Planning.* Exchange lists help people to eat a nutritionally balanced diet and include a wide variety of foods without having to count calories.

There are six exchange lists:

1. Starch/bread
2. Meat
3. Vegetable
4. Fruit
5. Milk
6. Fat

Exchange lists contain measured portions, or servings, of food which may be substituted, traded, or exchanged for other foods items within the same list. All of the foods on each list have similar amounts of carbohydrate, protein, fat, and calories. Specific serving sizes are listed for each food, and substitutes must be made in the amount specified.

People with diabetes use a meal plan to outline the number of exchanges from each food list to eat at meals and snacks. A meal plan is individualized according to a person's lifestyle, age, weight, sex, activity level, and whether or not medication is used to help control the diabetes. People who do not have diabetes may also use a meal plan to help ensure a balanced diet and maintain a consistent calorie intake each day.

To obtain an individualized meal plan using exchanges, contact a Registered Dietitian (R.D.) in your area. An R.D. can assess your current eating habits, recommend changes to help you achieve your nutritional goals, and determine an appropriate calorie level for you.

For more information on the Exchange Lists, write to the American Diabetes Association, Diabetes Information Service Center, 1660 Duke Street, Alexandria, Virginia 22314. Or write to the American Dietetic Association, 430 North Michigan Avenue, Chicago, Illinois 60611.